BETWEEN TWO WORLDS
Navigating "Italian" Studies in the United States

PAOLO A. GIORDANO

Edited and with an Introduction by
Anthony Julian Tamburri

Afterword by Fred L. Gardaphé

CASA LAGO PRESS
NEW FAIRFIELD, CT

Diaspora
Volume 10

As "diaspora" is the dispersion or spread of people from their original homeland, this book series takes its name in the intellectual spirit of willful dispersion of subject matter and thought. It is dedicated to publishing those studies and creative works that in various and sundry ways either speak to or offer new methods of analysis and/or articulations of the Italian diaspora.

The publication of this book has been made possible through a generous grant from an anonymous donor who wishes not to be identified but urges others to donate to historical and cultural studies.

COVER ART: "Bordighera" by Claude Monet (1884)
Potter Palmer Collection, Art Institute of Chicago

ISBN 978-1-955995-14-6
Library of Congress Control Number: Available upon request

© 2025 Paolo A. Giordano
© 2025 Authors

All rights reserved.
Printed in the United States of America

CASA LAGO PRESS
New Fairfield, CT

Table of Contents

Acknowledgements (vi)

"Introduction," Anthony Julian Tamburri (vii)

"Paolo A. Giordano, Curriculum vitae" (xvii)

Part I
1. "Italian Immigrant Literary Studies in the United States: An Orphan Child?" (3)
2. "Living on the Hyphen: Two Italian-Born Writers in the United States" (15)
3. "Forced Migration: Between Autobiography and Novel" (41)

Part II
4. "Gabriello Chiabrera: An Overview" (73)
5. "Beppe Fenoglio's Theatrical and Cinematic Writings: An Overview" (99)

Part III
6. Bernardino Ciambelli, "The Victim" (123)

Part IV
7. Friends (181)

Part V
8. Photos (225)

Afterword, Fred L. Gardaphé (231)

Index of Names (237)

Acknowledgements

As I have repeatedly stated in other venues, no essay or book, whatever its structure, is ever completed in a vacuum; there is always someone with whom we all share our ideas and inevitably who serves as our sounding board.

A few people have been instrumental in this case. First, when I initially thought of this homage, I spoke to Rosa Bellino Giordano, Paul's wife of more than fifty years. It seemed like a normal place to start. I then spoke to a few of our friends here about crafting a list. The idea behind such a list was to identify those individuals with whom at different periods in his career Paul had collaborated and as often happens in one's professional life, may have counseled and/or mentored. At this juncture, for names and for advice on the structure of this book, I am happy to thank, first and foremost, Rosa Bellino Giordano. As well, a heart-felt *grazie* also goes to Ryan Calabretta-Sajder, Chiara Mazzuchelli, and Mark Pietralunga. At the John D. Calandra Italian American Institute, I am always assisted by Sian Gibby and Nicholas Grosso; be it their copy-editing or book design, they are always ready to help. I sincerely thank them all for their keen insights and commentary.

The essays included in this book have appeared in different venues. They appear here with very slight editing, as is often the case in these situations. The inclusion was to choose essays that represent Paul's long and productive career. A professor of Italian by formation and trade, he also dedicated a good amount of his career to Italian/American studies, especially those writers who write in Italian. As the reader will see, he also engaged in the long-standing debate on labeling and categorization: who are these writers who have or continue to live in the United States and yet write in Italian. To represent further his intellectual work, Paul also engaged in translation. Here, we included his English rendition of Bernardino Ciambelli's "The Victim."

The essays included herein appeared in the following venues: "Italian Immigrant Literary Studies in the United States: An Orphan Child?" in Anthony Julian Tamburri and Fred Gardaphé, eds. *Transcending Borders, Bridging Gaps. Italian Americana, Diasporic Studies, and the University Curriculum* (New York: Calandra Institute, 2015): 68-74; "Living on the Hyphen: Two Italian-Born Writers in the United States" in Sian Gibby, Joseph Sciorra, Anthony Julian Tamburri, eds. *This Hope Sustains the Scholar: Essays in Tribute to the Work of Robert Viscusi* (Bordighera 2021): 161-180; "Forced Migration: Between Autobiography and Novel" appeared in Italian in "L'emigrazione coatta: tra autobiografia e romanzo" in Anthony Julian Tamburri and Paolo A. Giordano, eds. *Esilio, migrazione, sogno americano. Italiana* X (2002): 93-111; "Gabriello Chiabrera: An Overview" is a slightly edited version of his entry, "Gabriello Chiabrera," in Albert Mancini and Glenn Palen Pierce, eds. *Seventeenth Century Italian Poetry Volume of the Dictionary of Literary Biographies*. Gale Press, 2008; "Beppe Fenoglio's Theatrical and Cinematic Writings: An Overview" in Paolo Giordano and Anthony Julian Tamburri, eds. *Essays in Honor of Albert Mancini*, a special issue of *Italiana* VIII (1999): 146-156; the translation of Bernardino Ciambelli, "The Victim (La vittima)" in *Italoamericana: The Literature of the Great migration, 1880-1943*. Ed. Francesco Durante. New York: Fordham UP, 2014: 167-202.

Introduction

Professional Lives in a Parallel Universe

> *The challenge of modernity is to live without illusions and without becoming disillusioned. I'm a pessimist because of intelligence, but an optimist because of will.*
> ANTONIO GRAMSCI

The idea to organize a volume in honor of Paul (Paolo) Giordano came to me some time ago, but I waited to be sure that all pieces were in place for all involved; nothing in particular, only to be sure that the proverbial stars were aligned.

As some of you may know, Paul and I grew up together in Stamford, Connecticut; and it is for this reason that what follows is imbued with the personal and thus not the typical encomium one might expect to find in these venues. While most friendships in our academic world begin with the professional and move to the personal, ours began in early adolescence.

I was born In Stamford; Paul and his family came from Italy when he was nine years old. Obviously, he was Paolo on arrival, but we all knew him as Paul, as was the case with many immigrants at that time, their names being Americanized once they entered school and began to befriend their schoolmates.

At that time, being a year older, Paul was first friends more with my older brother and his friends than with me and my friends. That one year was a notable chasm back then. Nonetheless, that one-year difference was also a small gap readily bridged in school. Paul and I were part of the first rounds of busing back in the first half of the 1960s,[1] and we attended a new high school, Rippowam, which opened its doors in 1961 in the "northern part" of town that was not ethnically mixed. In a report prepared in 1977 by the Connecticut Advisory Committee to the U.S. Commission on Civil Rights, we read that there was a "racial and socioeconomic imbalance at the two schools (145 of 157 black high school students were at Stamford High) and in a majority report the committee recommended that a north-south district line be established for Stamford High School and Rippowam." As we read, there were twelve Black students not enrolled at Stamford High School all of which means that they were most likely divided between one public (Rippowam) and one private high school (Stamford Catholic High School).[2]

I offer this brief history of the racial and ethnic make-up of Stamford's secondary-school population of the time precisely because it was the social context in which Paul and I grew up and attended high school. The local NAACP, in fact, underscored the importance of desegregation at this time, seeing it as the opportunity for students from both sides of the divide "to develop into fully rounded adults by associ-

---

[1] "Stamford began voluntarily racially desegregating schools in the early 1960s. In 1962, Stamford's Board of Education developed a plan to desegregate the district's two high schools" (Potter).

[2] Said the NAACP at the time: "If the proposed districting were allowed to stand, the school population of Rippowam High School would be overwhelmingly white and from economically privileged homes. This is harmful not only to the children who live in the southern part of the city, but equally harmful to children of the northern part of Stamford, for they shall be deprived of the opportunity to develop into fully rounded adults by association with people of diverse background and cultures."

ation with people of diverse background and cultures" (Anonymous 1961, 25). Paul and I were indeed afforded this opportunity in 1963 and 1964, our first years of high school.

This newly recognized racial and ethnic social context surely formed us two as individuals, making us consciously aware of the diverse racial and ethnic background of the United States. Until then, we lived in our local, Italian/American neighborhood on the "West Side" of Stamford, where most "Italians" lived.[3] Being bused to a high school where not only was it predominantly White, but we were, to some degree, part of a new fascinating, if you will, student population. We were Blacks, Italians, Puerto Ricans, and members of other racial and ethnic groups coming from the west and southern parts of Stamford. Further still, and more significant I would contend, it made us more cognizant of such divides as we moved forward in our professional lives and found ourselves on both sides of the academic Italian divide between "real Italians" and Italian Americans.[4]

Having graduated from high school — and with Paul having taken a short detour to New Britain, Connecticut — we ended up at Southern Connecticut State College in Fall 1967 in New Haven.[5] Both Italian majors, we spent four years engaged in athletics, cultural programs, and the Italian club only to graduate in 1971 and continue our studies in Middlebury College's M.A. program in Florence, Italy.

---

[3] For Italian in quotes, see my "The Semiotics of Labeling" (2019) and Ruberto and Sciorra's "Introduction" (2017).
[4] For my use of the adjective "real," see Ruberto and Sciorra. See also my ""The Coincidence of Italian Cultural Hegemonic Privilege" (2017).
[5] In March 1983, Southern Connecticut State College became Southern Connecticut State University.

June 1971 • Graduation, Southern Connecticut State College
Asst. Dean Michael Dante, Paul, Anthony

At the time of our graduation from Southern Connecticut State College, Middlebury's M.A. in Florence was the only program in which the American student was enrolled alongside the local Italian students in the Università degli Studi di Firenze, we too having to go through the public oral exam experience, with, for at least one course, close to one hundred students present, listening to the possible questions they too might have to answer.

The Middlebury experience was in many ways a formative period for the both of us. We each realized that studying and eventually teaching Italian literature and culture could be a pleasurable and productive profession at the university level. So, we each applied to PhD programs, Paul ending up at Indiana University and I at the University of California.

As our high-school and college years mirrored each other, so has our professional lives. We were in constant collaboration over the years. We organized conferences, we co-edited books together and with others as well. One experience that also solidified our working experience was the American Association of Teachers of Italian. We were each vice-president and president: Paul was VP for the two years 2004-2006, the president form 2006-2008; I, in turn, was vice-president during his presidency, 2006-2008, and president from 2008-2010. Our respective presidencies were very much involved with the Advanced Placement Program in Italian (AP). During Paul's time, the AP was instituted in 2004. During my time, we had to confront the initial crisis and its suspension.[6] Today, the AP is very much alive, and its numbers are steady for the most part.

In addition to our childhood-born friendship, the activity that kept us in touch almost daily for most of our professional decades was publishing. Beyond the borders of the world of university presses, Paul was one of the initial innovators in publishing. Having established a relationship with Albert Mancini in the mid-1980s, when Paul was still at Rosary College (now, Dominican University), the publication *Italiana* was born, and it exists still today as a publication of Bordighera Press.[7] The trinity behind that project

---

[6] For more on the history of the AP in Italian, see Roberto Dolci.

[7] The first scholarly press beyond the world of the university press here in North America seems to have been Studia Humanitatis (1973), which eventually morphed into Scripta Humanistica. In 1986, Gradiva Publications was born. A year later in 1987, Leonard Sbrocchi founded Legas in Ottawa, Canada, with Gaetano Cipolla as the New York counterpart. Dedicated primarily to the creative work with ample scholarly titles as well, Guernica Editions was founded in 1978 by Antonio D'Alfonso. In

was Albert Mancini, Piero Baldini, and Paul. Until the birth of Bordighera Press, Rosary College was the sponsoring entity behind *Italiana*.

At about the time Bordighera Press was born, Albert Mancini became editor of *Italica*, the official organ of the American Association of Teachers of Italian. He invited both Paul and me to serve as associate editors, which we did for Mancini's two terms. This was during the initial years of Bordighera Press, and our collaboration with Mancini was most formative, I would submit.

In February 1987, Paul, Fred Gardaphe, and I attended the University of Louisville's 20th Century Literature Conference. We did a panel on Italian/American writers; it was, we believe, the first time such a session was held. Most uncanny of this experience was the public's reaction to the concept of the session, writers of Italian origin labeled as Italian American; the actual presentations seemed to have been of secondary interest. With an audience of more than fifty people — most Italian Americans and most professors of anything but Italian — the first observation, indeed accusation, was that we were doing a great disservice to these writers by labeling them "Italian American." They were, after all, we were told with much conviction, "American"!

North America, these are the first independent presses at the foreground of the academic, scholarly, and creative world of publishing within the last thirty years of the twentieth century. There was academic publishing, in English, happening earlier in Italy. But that phenomenon has its own vicissitudes that are better discussed in another venue and at greater length than a footnote can provide.

From that day on in February 1987, several things were born; it proved to be an important encounter for a variety of reasons. First, while Paul and Fred had already known each other as fellow Chicagoans, it was a first encounter for Fred and me. We went on to become, as Giose Rimanelli baptized us, "I ragazzi di Chicago." Our first venture as this new trinity was the compilation of our anthology, *From the Margin: Writings in Italian Americana*. We felt it was important to document what we had done in Louisville and what we thought was the significance of the project; this was especially true for both Paul and Fred, who had been working in this field notably earlier than me. I, in turn, was just getting my feet wet in this field.

From our work on the anthology, the journal *Voices in Italian Americana* (VIA) was born, for which we then created Boridghera Incorporated, a 501(3) non-profit organization. Having then published in the early 1990s the first few books in a series we had created as *VIA* FOLIOS, we realized that the moniker "Press" sounded better than "Incorporated." And thus, Boridghera Press was born!

With thirty-five years of service, Boridghera Press has published *Voices in Italian Americana* beginning in 1990. Since 1992, it has amassed a list of close to 300 books and special issues of *Italiana*. It has been a collaboration of the three of us: what is good, what is not good; what to publish, what not to publish. In addition to the numbers, our books have won numerous awards, and our authors span the globe. Equally satisfying is that we have also published several scholars who then went on to earn tenure.

This is Bordighera Press: two journals, hundreds of books published, and, as its mission states, activities dedicated to the promotion of both the Italian and Italian/American cultures. This is what Paul has helped to build in no small way. His voice was then, at the beginning, and remains still today, wise and instrumental in how we move forward. It is his signature, uncannily so, that sealed the deal for the passage of Bordighera Press to become part of the John D. Calandra Italian American Institute.

This handful selection of Paul's scholarly work demonstrates the breadth of his intellectual interests. It also underscores his desire to connect the Italian to the Italian/American cultural world. Among the very few in the 1980s, Paul was in the forefront of this enterprise. This is especially evident in the essays "Living on the Hyphen" and "Forced Migration," in which he discusses not only the Italian-born, as he does in the former, but the first-generation writer as well in the latter.

Given the time and place of where we grew up and how we were eventually formed as the individuals we have become, we have often marveled at our successes, as small as they may seem within the greater scheme of things. One of my cousins occasionally reminds me with the abbreviation, FFFA, *Far from Fairfield Avenue*, which was the street where I spent the first nine years of my life. Together, Paul and I can slightly modify my cousin's reminder into FFSC, *Far from Stamford, Connecticut*. Not that we wanted to leave, but our professional lives brought us to where we are today.

So, in closing this parallel/personal overview of Paul's successful career, it seemed most appropriate to honor him with this publication of a third iteration that is Casa Lago Press, which has its origins in Bordighera Press, which, in turn, has its origins in *Italiana*, that publication first created by Paul and company back in the 1980s!

REFERENCES

Anonymous. 1977. "School Desegregation in Stamford, Connecticut." Connecticut Advisory Committee to the U.S. Commission on Civil Rights. Dated, July 1977. PDF.

Anonymous. 1961. "Statement submitted to Board of Education." National Association for the Advancement of Colored People. June 29. Cited in Anonymous (1977, 25).

Dolci, Roberto. 2023. *Advanced Placement Program in Italian: History and Analysis.* New York: John D. Calandra Italian American Institute.

Potter, Halley. 2016. "Stamford Public Schools: From Desegregated Schools to Integrated Classrooms." *The Century Foundation.* October 14. https://tcf.org/content/report/ stamford-public-schools/#:~:text=Stamford%20began%20voluntaily% 20racially%20desegregaing,points%20of%20the%20district %20average. Accessed March 6, 2025.

Ruberto, Laura and Joseph Sciorra, eds. 2017. "Introduction." In *New Italian Migrations to the United States, Vol. 1: Politics and History since 1945.* Chicago: University of Illinois Press. 1-32.

Tamburri, Anthony Julian. 2017. "The Coincidence of Italian Cultural Hegemonic Privilege and the Historical Amnesia of Italian Diaspora Articulations." In *Re-Mapping Italian America. Places, Cultures, Identities*, Sabrina Vellucci and Carla Francellini, eds. New York: Bordighera. 53-76.

Tamburri, Anthony Julian. 2019. "The Semiotics of Labeling: 'Italian' to 'American,' 'Non-white' to 'White,' and Other Privileges of Choosing." In Susanna Nanni and Sabrina Vellucci, eds. *Circolazione di persone e di idee.* New York: Bordighera Press. 1-18.

Neil R. Euliano Distinguished Professor, 2008–2018

PAOLO GIORDANO

EDUCATION
Indiana University – Doctor of Philosophy (1978) in Italian Literature; minor area of specialization in Art History
Middlebury College – Master of Arts in Italian (1972); Università di Firenze (1971-72);
Southern Connecticut State University – Bachelor of Arts (1971); Major, Italian; Minor, Spanish.

ACADEMIC POSITIONS HELD
UNIVERSITY OF CENTRAL FLORIDA
2004–2018 – Neil R. Euliano Professor of Italian
Chair, Department of Modern Languages and Literatures: 2004-2014
Director, Summer Program in Florence: May/June 2008, 2010, 2011, 2013
LOYOLA UNIVERSITY/CHICAGO
Chair, Department of Modern Languages & Literatures: 1998 – 2004
Director, Graduate Program of Liberal Studies: 1993-1994.
Director and Academic Dean (Associate Dean College of Arts and Sciences), Loyola University/Chicago Rome Campus: 1989–1992.
Director Loyola Summer Program in Italy, 1994-1997
MIDDLEBURY COLLEGE
Italian School. 1988, 1989, 1993, 1995, 2002, 2009
ROSARY COLLEGE, 1977-1989
SOUTHEASTERN LOUISIANA UNIVERSITY.1975-1976 Instructor.
TANGIPAHOA PARISH SCHOOL BOARD, Amite Louisiana–1975-1977 – Bilingual Specialist and Testing Director

ADMINISTRATIVE POSITIONS HELD
UNIVERSITY OF CENTRAL FLORIDA
Chair, Dept. of Modern Languages and Literatures: 2004–2014.
Director, Summer Program in Florence: 2008, 2010, 2011, 2013.

LOYOLA UNIVERSITY
    Chair, Department of Modern Languages and Literatures: 1998 – 2004
    Director, Master of Arts in Liberal Studies: 1993–1994.
    Director and Academic Dean (Associate Dean College of Arts and Sciences), Loyola University/Chicago Rome Campus: 1989–1992.
    Director Loyola Summer Program in Italy, 1994–1997.
ROSARY COLLEGE
    Director, International Studies Program 1987-1989.
    Director & Founder, Rosary Summer Program in Florence 1980–1988.

HONORS & AWARDS

Emeritus Professor, April 2019.

Received the "Parmurelu d'oru" lifetime achievement award from the Descu Rundu Cultural Association of Bordighera, Italy, 2012.

Appointed Neil R. Euliano Distinguished Professor, August 2008.

"Cavaliere, Stella della Solidarietà Italiana" Honor bestowed by the President of the Republic of Italy through the Consulate General office of Chicago, Illinois, June 2004.

Outstanding Alumnus Award, Southern Connecticut State University, May 2004.

Recipient of Outstanding Service Award from the Illinois Foreign Language Teachers Association, 1986.

PUBLICATIONS
BOOKS

From the Margin: Writings in Italian Americana. (Second and Revised Edition) Edited with Anthony Julian Tamburri and Fred L. Gardaphé. Purdue University Press, 1991 (2nd Ed. 2000). Introduction, essay and bibliography.

Beyond the Margin: Further Writings in Italian Americana. Edited with Anthony Julian Tamburri. Fairleigh Dickinson UP, 1997. Introduction, essay, and bibliography

Joseph Tusiani: Poet, Translator, Humanist an International Homage. Paolo Giordano, ed. Bordighera Press, 1994.

The Hyphenate Writer and the Legacy of Exile. Paolo Giordano, ed. Bordighera Press, 2010.

Introducing Italian Americana: generalities on Literature and Film. A bilingual forum. Bordighera Press, 2006

Esilio Migrazione e Sogno Americano. Edited with Anthony Julian Tamburri. W. Lafayette: Bordighera Press, 2001. Introduction and Essay.

Pluralism and Critical Practice: Essays in Honor of Albert Mancini. Edited with Anthony Julian Tamburri. *Italiana VIII*. Bordighera Press, 1999. Introduction and essay

L'esilio come certezza: La ricerca d'identità culturale in Italia dalla rivoluzione francese ai nostri giorni. Edited with Andrea Ciccarelli. *Italiana VII*. W. Lafayette: Bordighera Press, 1998. Introduction and essay.

Test Bank for *Oggi in Italia* (1st year text). Co-Author Rosa Bellino-Giordano. New York: Houghton-Mifflin, 1982. 1-186.

TRANSLATIONS

Ciambelli, Bernardino. "The Victim (La vittima)" in *Italoamericana: The Literature of the Great migration, 1880-1943*. Francesco Durante, ed. Fordham UP, 2014: 167-202.

Vacirca, Vincezo. "The Fire" (Il rogo) in *Italoamericana: The Literature of the Great migration, 1880-1943*. Francesco Durante, ed. Fordham UP, 2014: 697-708.

ARTICLES (Selected)

"Living on the Hyphen: Two Italian-Born Writers in the United States" in Sian Gibby, Joseph Sciorra, Anthony Julian Tamburri, eds. *This Hope Sustains the Scholar: Essays in Tribute to the Work of Robert Viscusi*. Bordighera Press, 2021. 161-180.

"Joseph Tusiani at Ninety: The Man and his Work." *ITALICA*, 93.2 (2016): 318-337.

"Studi letterari su scrittori immigranti negli Stati Uniti: Figlio orfano? *Palinsesti*, Calabria (Italy). Spring 2015.

"Italian Immigrant Literary Studies in the United States: Orphan Child?" in *Transcending Borders, Bridging Gaps: Italian Americana, Diasporic Studies and the University Curriculum*. New York: Calandra Institute, 2014: 68-74.

"Images of America and Columbus as Part of the Mosaic of American Identity" International Conference *American Cultural Myths and Perspectives on the USA Literary Perception*. Moscow, Russia, 2012

"Gabriello Chiabrera" *Literary Encyclopedia*. London. 2011.

"The Legacy of Exile: Italian Writers in the United States." *International Conference, American Cultural Myths and Perspectives on the USA Literary Perception*. Moscow Russia, 2010.

"Quando gli albanesi eravamo noi" Proceedings of the International Conference *Ri-narrare il meridione*. Erice, Italy, May 27–31, 2009.

"Gabriello Chiabrera." *Seventeenth Century Italian Poetry Volume of the Dictionary of Literary Biographies*. Dictionary of Italian Literary Biographies: Gale Press, 2008.

"La voce femminile nella narrativa italo-americana." Proceedings of the International Conference L'emigrazione Siciliana nel Nuovo Mondo (Sec. XVIII-XX)." University of Messina (Sicily).

"Chiaro Davanzati" *Encyclopedia of Italian Literature*. New York: Routledge: 2007.

"Gabriello Chiabrera." *Encyclopedia of Italian Literature*. New York: Routledge: 2007.

"La narrativa italo americana: un escursione storica." *Esilio Migrazione e Sogno Americano*. 2001.

"Beppe Fenoglio's Theatrical and Cinematic Writings: An Overview" *Essays in Honor of Albert Mancini, Italiana VIII*, 1999.

"Tra autobiografia e romanzo: L'emigrazione coatta nelle opere di Pascal D'Angelo, Guido D'Agostino, Helen Barolini, and Joseph Tusiani" *Il sogno italo-americano. Realtà e immaginario dell'emigrazione negli Stati Uniti. Atti del Convegno "Il sogno italo-americano."* 28-30 Nov. 1996. Sebastiano Martelli, ed. Napoli: Suor Orsola Benincasa, 1998. 89-108.

"Dall'Italia all'America: *I quattro camminanti* di Rodolfo di Biasio" *L'esilio come certezza: La ricerca d'identità culturale in Italia dalla rivoluzione francese ai nostri giorni.* W. Lafayette: Bordighera Press, 1998: 149-161.

"Emigranti, espatriati e/o esiliati:Italiani e letteratura negli Stati Uniti." *Lo Straniero.* Eds. Mario Domenichelli and Pino Fasano. Roma: Bulzoni Editore, 1998: 169-184.

"Emigrants, Expatriates and/or Exiles: Italian Writing in America." *Beyond the Margin: Further Writings in Italian Americana.* Paul A. Giordano and Anthony J. Tamburri, eds. Rutheford, NJ: Fairleigh Dickinson UP, December 1997: 223-241.

"Tusiani and the Saga of Immigration." *Joseph Tusiani: Poet, Translator, Humanist.* Bordighera Press, 1994.

"1990, L'estate rovente di Cesare Pavese." *Romance Language Annual*, Vol. 6, 1994.

"The Writer Suspended Between Two Worlds: Joseph Tusiani's *Autobiografia di un italo-americano*." *Differentia* 6 (1994)..

"Images of America and Columbus in Italian/American Literature." *Annali d'Italianistica* 10 (1992).

"From Italian Emigrant to Reluctant American: Joseph Tusiani's *Gente Mia and Other Poems*." In *From the Margin. Writings in Italian Americana.* Purdue UP, 1991.

"Dai margini al centro: lo scrittore italiano/ americano" *Campi Immaginabili*, I, 2. Formerly *Ipotesi '80.*

"La poesia di Paolo Foglietta e la Genova del '500" *Italiana* 1987.

"Italian Immigration to the State of Louisiana: Causes, Effects and Results." *Italian Americana*, Spring (1979): 160-177.

"Il Cristo in Pietà: Un Taddeo di Bartolo trascurato." *Commentari* (Rome, 1974). Translation from the English to Italian.

BIBLIOGRAPHIES:

"The Calandra Italian American and Italian Diaspora Studies Bibliography," with Stephen J. Cerulli. https://calandrainstitute.org/research-and-education/the-calandra-italian-american-and-italian-diaspora-studies-bibliography/

"Italian Studies in North America" *Italica* 1994- 2004 (Summer and Winter issues)

"Bibliografia rimanelliana" *Festschrift in Honor of Giose Rimanelli. Fililibri*, a publication of *Forum Italicum* (SUNY Stony Brook),1999.

"Italian American Bibliography" (poetry, prose, and critical works) in *From the Margins: Writings in Italian Americana.* Purdue UP, 1991. Update in 2000 for second edition.

EDITORIAL EXPERIENCE

Associate Editor, *Italica*, the journal of the American Association of Teachers of Italian. 1994- 2003.

Co-Editor and Co-founder with Anthony Tamburri and Fred Gardaphé of *Voices in Italian Americana: a literary and cultural review* a journal of ethnic studies. 1990—

Co-Editor of the American Italian Historical Association's Conference proceedings. 1987 and 2007

Editor of the AATI Newsletter (1985–1987).

Co-founder with Piero Baldini and Albert Mancini. *Italiana.* 1987—

MEMBERSHIP IN PROFESSIONAL ORGANIZATIONS

American Association of Teachers of Italian
American Association of Italian Studies
American Italian Historical Association
Renaissance Society of America
Midwest Modern Language Association
Multi-Ethnic Literatures of the United States (MELUS)

Part I

Italian Americana

Italian Immigrant Literary Studies in the United States: An Orphan Child?

Except for a few pages on Helen Barolini's *Umbertina*, and a few other Italian American writers born in the United States who expressed themselves in English, I have, in the past, strictly dealt with Italian immigrant writers. In Italian-American Studies my name is mostly tied to Joseph Tusiani, having written a number of articles on his poetry and the autobiographical trilogy, *La parola difficile, La parola nuova,* e *La parola antica*. I have also worked on Italian writers who addressed the issue of emigration and who gave us the perspective of those who remained behind, and the hardships that emigration wrought on Italian families and frequently on whole villages and towns: Some of the texts that come to mind are *Sull'Oceano* by Edmondo de Amicis which gives us a first-hand account of what it was like to cross the ocean in steerage; Giovanni Pascoli's poem "Italy," dedicated to a theme dear to Pascoli, that Italian emigrants forced painfully to abandon their home to seek a better life in another country; Luigi Pirandello's "L'altro figlio," a short story from his collection *Novelle per un anno,* and popularized by the Taviani brothers in their film *Kaos*; Rodolfo di Biasio's short novel *I quattro camminanti,* a novel derived from the hundreds of letters that four brothers, the "quattro camminanti" of the title mailed, over the years, to their mother in Italy.[1]

Given my research preferences I was really quite pleased when I received my assignment for the Bellagio conference—"Italian Immigrant Literary Studies in the U.S.: An Orphan Child?" Italian immigrant writing is a topic that is central to my research interests.

The quick and very short answer to the question posed to me is a resounding YES, Italian Immigrant writing has, until recently, been almost forgotten. These foundational texts are not read and are not taught in the various classes and programs of Italian and Italian-American studies in the U.S. One of the reasons for the current state of affairs is that most of the books from this early period are out of print and not available. Just as important, do scholars and teachers of Italian and Italian-American Studies literature think that these writers are important to the "program"?

These thousands of novels, poems, plays, biographies, autobiographies, journals, dailies and other forms of expression written in Italian are important, amazingly so, if we want to fully understand the migration experience and the formation, or creation, of an "Italian-American" identity or, more accurately, identities. As a number of the colleagues present at the

---

[1] For further information on Italian writers and emigration see,: Francesco De Nicola.

Bellagio conference/workshop pointed out, we are not a homogenous group. Our experiences are different. Of the nine colleagues present that came from the United States three emigrated to the United States between 1957 and 1963, two emigrated much later, and four are second- and third-generation Italian American. We all have different experiences and, I venture to say, we all have lived, and live our hyphenated identity differently.[2]

Mary Jo Bona wrote, "Perhaps it is our fortune that we do not possess a single definition of ourselves." To expand and complete the definition of "ourselves" we need to look at the whole picture and, obviously, that includes the writings of our Italian immigrant forebears.

Throughout the nineteenth and twentieth century the myth of America attracted millions of Italians to its shore, among them literary critics, mainstream writers and intellectuals. Some came for short visits and wrote about their travels and perceptions, though limited they may have been. Among them, the literary critic Emilio Cecchi's *America amara,* the futurist Fortunato Depero's *Un futurista a New York* (notes published posthumously), Mario Soldati's *America primo amore,* and Goffredo Parise's *Odore d'America* come to mind. Others, like Giuseppe Prezzolini, stayed longer and their

---

[2] See Fred L, Gardaphé's "Identical Difference: Notes on Italian and Italian-American Identities."

impact was more lasting. Giuseppe Prezzolini, Professor of Italian at Columbia University and director of its Casa Italiana, was a missionary of Italian culture and a highly respected intellectual who, during his stay in America wrote, among other things, *I trapiantati* (1953), *America in pantofole* (1950), *America con gli stivali* (1954) and an interesting article "America and Italy: Myths and Realities." (*Italian Quarterly* [Spring 1959]).

Along with these Italian literati, a generation of writers, journalists, playwrights, political and religious activists and exiles emigrated whose purpose was to make the New World their home. Bernardino Ciambelli (1862–1931) was a journalist, author of novels and plays, and also an actor and "capocomico." His novels not only tell stories about Italian immigrants they also describe the city of New York at the end of the 19th century and the first decades of the 20th: the undergrounds, the multi-ethnic neighborhoods, Chinatown, The Irish brothels, Little Italy, and other details of life.[3] Samuel Charles Mazzuchelli, O.P. (1806–1864) a pioneer Italian Catholic missionary who brought the church to the Iowa-Illinois-Wisconsin tristate area. He founded a number of parishes in the area and was the architect for a number of parish buildings. Among his many contributions, Mazzucchelli translated a catechism into the Winnebago language, and published an almanac in the Chippewa language. Pasquale (Pascal)

---

[3] See Francesco Durante (2013).

D'Angelo came to the United States at the age of 16. While working as a laborer and living under brutal conditions he taught himself English and began to write poetry. Soon his poems were published in important literary journals such as *The Literary Review*, *The Nation*, and *The New York Times*. In 1924, he published his autobiography *Son of Italy* where this "pick and shovel" worker, as he describes himself, narrates the harsh, almost inhumane, conditions that he and other immigrants suffered. Riccardo Cordiferro, baptized Alessandro Sisca, was a poet, essayist, playwright, historical scholar, anarchist who spent a number of years in jail for his political activity. He was the founder of *La Follia di New York*, a magazine whose life spanned a century, and the author of a popular Neapolitan song, "Core 'ngrato." These are but a few examples of the many that are documented in Rose Basile Green's groundbreaking work *The Italian-American Novel* and Francesco Durante's monumental *Italoamericana: The Literature of the great Migration 1880-1943*.

Beginning with the nineteen-nineties we have witnessed the beginning of a fertile period for the scholarship of the early period of Italian immigrant writing. Francesco Durante, journalist for "Il mattino" of Naples and Professor at the University Suor Orsola Benincasa published an enormous two volume critical study and anthology titled *Italoamericana* published by Mondadori: the first tome is about the literature of

Italians that emigrated to the U.S.A. from 1776 to 1880 (2001); the second book deals with the literature of the period that spans the "great migration" from 1880 and 1943 (2005). This second volume was translated and published by Fordham University Press this past year. Durante's monumental study was followed by two excellent studies by Martino Marazzi, *Voices of Italian America* and *A occhi aperti: letteratura dell'emigrazione e mito Americano*. Marazzi's studies trace the cultural history of Italian immigrants during the first half of the twentieth century and offer the reader a path to understanding the fabrication of Italian-American history and culture. As important as the historical, and literary and cultural analysis is, the most valuable contribution of Marazzi's book is the anthology, which gave new life to the works of numerous writers that most of us have not read and most likely had never heard their names. To these ground-breaking studies we must add Ilaria Serra's study *The Value of Worthless Lives* that, for the first time, explores the "mostly unpublished, often thickly accented, tales of ordinary men and women . . . to reflect (their) realities of work, survival, identity, and change." To these studies, one must also include Jim Pericone's excellent annotated bibliography *Strangers in a Strange Land. A Survey of Italian-language American Imprints* (1830–1945). This wonderful book catalogues the Italian-language book-publishing industry that began in the nineteenth century and flourished in the United States in the fifty years before World War II.

This early period comes to an end in the years immediately following World War II. As Martino Marazzi states in the above mentioned *Voices of Italian America,* "The Italian-America that speaks and writes Italian, or its dialects, in the literary sense has disappeared forever." One could say that this period ends with Joseph Tusiani,[4] one of the last of this group who with eloquence and dignity addressed the experience of immigration to the United States in his Italian-American trilogy written in Italian, *La parola difficile, La parola nuova* and *La parola antica,* with the collective subtitle *Autobiografia di un italo-americano.* In the 958 pages of the trilogy, Tusiani not only narrates his life and that of his family from the day he landed in New York in 1947, he also takes us on a voyage through the history of Italian migration to the United States. Many of the people, some famous others not, that grace the pages of this work constitute the essence of this migration.

Since the 1950s we have witnessed a second wave of writers from Italy who produced, and continue to produce a substantial amount of poetry and prose both in the Italian language and in the English language. The list is long: Joseph Tusiani, Giose Rimanelli, Peter Carravetta, Gianna Patriarca, Frances Winwar

---

[4] See Marazzi (2004) and Giordano (1998).

(Francesca Vinciguerra) Luigi Fontanella, Paolo Valesio, Luigi Ballerini, Rita Dinale, Alessandro Carrera, and Emanuele Pettener are some of the more prominent names. Through their writing a distinctive American voice in Italian literature, or maybe an Italian voice in American literature is starting to define itself. These writers have given a new voice to Italian America, and, by their form and content, they give recognition to the fact that Italian America is neither monolingual nor monocultural.[5] Unfortunately, many of these books suffered the same fate as those of their predecessors and quickly went out of print.

The studies mentioned above have given us a clearer understanding of the literary production and cultural history of that period of mass migration and indicate a path to follow. We now also have a book, Marazzi's *Voices of Italian America* that can be used as a text in a university course on early Italian immigrant writing. What is needed now is to build on these studies and, more importantly, create a curriculum to bring this information to the classroom, if not, this knowledge will continue to remain the domain of the few. To bring this knowledge to our students a conscientious effort is needed to rescue these writings from the dustbin of history and find a way to have at least a

---

[5] See Anthony Julian Tamburri (1991), Peter Carravetta (1991), and Paolo Valesio (1993). On Italian writers in America see also Anthony Julian Tamburri (2014) and Paolo Giordano (1997).

number of these books republished in the original Italian and translated into English, either in traditional book form or digitized. This, as many of you know, is a long and tedious process and for anything to be accomplished one needs grant money, time and a team of scholars to work on it together, I am also thinking of graduate students who could turn some of this work into dissertations and publications. I have begun working with the Digital Humanities Center at my university to see what can be done, what roads to take and what strategies to develop.

Giuseppe Prezzolini was quoted as saying that Italian immigrants left behind tears and sweat but not words, living their lives in America mostly in silence, their memories private and stories untold. The studies that have been published in the recent past prove Prezzolini wrong, but unless we bring this wealth of knowledge to the classroom and disseminate it to our students and to a more general public, these voices will once again descend into oblivion.

BIBLIOGRAPHY

Basile Green, Rose. *The Italian American Novel: An Interaction of Two Cultures.* Madison, NJ: Fairleigh Dickenson University Press, 1974.

Carravetta, Peter. "Concept, Direction, Introduction" to "Poessay VI: Voices from the Italian Diaspora." in *Romance Language Notes* II (1991)

D'Angelo, Pascal. *Son of Italy: The autobiography of Pascal D'Angelo.* Toronto: Guernica Press,

De Nicola, Francesco. *Gli scrittori italiani e l'emigrazione* (Formia: Ghenoma s.r.l, .

Durante, Francesco. Interview in the magazine, *We the Italians* published October 24, 2013.

Durante, Francesco. *Italoamericana: The Literature of the great Migration 1880-1947*. Milano: Mondadori, 2005.

Fontanella, Luigi. *La Parola Trasfuga*. Fiesole: Edizioni Cadmi, 2003.

Gardaphé, Fred L. "Identical Difference: Notes on Italian and Italian-American Identities," in *The Essence of Italian Culture and the Challenge of a Global Age. Cultural Heritage and Contemporary Change*. Ed. George McClean and Piero Bassetti Series IV, West Europe (Series IV, West Europe, Volume 5). The Council for Research in Values and Philosophy, 2003. 93-112.

Giordano, Paul. "Emigrants, Expatriates and/or Exiles: Italian Writing in America." *Beyond the Margin: Further Writings in Italian Americana*. Eds. Paul A. Giordano and Anthony Julian Tamburri. Rutheford, NJ: Fairleigh Dickinson University Press, December 1997.

Giordano, Paul. "Tra autobiografia e romanzo: Il sogno italo-americano. Realtà e immaginario dell'emigrazione negli Stati Uniti. *Atti del Convegno "Il sogno italo-americano" 28-30 novembre 1996*. A cura di Sebastiano Martelli. Napoli: Suor Orsola Benincasa, 1998. 89-108.

Marazzi, Martino. *A occhi aperti: letteratura dell'emigrazione e mito American*. Milano: Franco Angeli Editore 2011.

Marazzi, Martino. *Voices of Italian America: A History of Early Italian American Literature with a Critical Anthology*. Fordham University Press, 2011.

Periconi, James J. *Strangers in a Strange Land. A Survey of Italian-language American Imprints (1830-1945*. New York: Bordighera Press, 2013.

Serra, Ilaria. *The Value of Worthless Lives: Writing Italian Immigrant Autobiographies*. New York: Fordham University Press, 2007.

Tamburri, Anthony Julian. "Identità 'italiana': Ovvero lo scrittore italiano all'estero." *Meditations on Identity-Meditazioni su identità*. Ed. Anthony Julian Tamburri. New York: Bordighera Press, 2014. 51-64.

Tamburri, Anthony Julian. Editor's Note to "Poessay VI: Voices from the Italian Diaspora." in *Romance Language Notes* II (1991).

Tusiani, Joseph. *La Parola Antica Autobiografia di un italo-americano*. Bari: Schena Editore, 1992.

Tusiani, Joseph. *La Parola Difficile Autobiografia di un italo-americano*. Bari: Schena Editore, 1988.

Tusiani, Joseph. *La Parola Nuova Autobiografia di un italo-americano*. Bari: Schena Editore, 1991.

Valesio, Paolo. "Introduction" *Poesaggio: Poeti italiani d'america*. Peter Carravetta & Paolo Valesio, eds. Quinto di Treviso: Pagus, 1993.

April 2019: Paul receives "Emeritus" status, the honorary title bestowed upon individuals, at retirement, recognizing their distinguished service.

Living on the Hyphen: Two Italian-Born Writers in the United States

> Di tutte le lontananze, l'America è la più vera ed esemplare.
> —Mario Soldati, *America primo amore*

Today several writers born and culturally trained in Italy live in the United States and write in Italian and English.[1] The list is long and their writing has defined itself as a distinctive American voice in Italian literature and/or an Italian voice in American literature and by their form and content recognizes the fact that Italian America is neither monolingual nor monocultural.

On the phenomenon of Italian American culture and its different aspects as manifested through its literature, Paolo Valesio (1989) states the following:

> The confusing codes, registers, genres (be they literary or cultural) often lead to reciprocal misunderstandings .... It becomes necessary, therefore, to distinguish between the following:

---

[1] Regarding the title of this essay: Perez-Firmat's (1994) *Life on the Hyphen* explores the "1.5 Generation" of Cubans that lived on the hyphen, neither one or the other but a fertile hybrid of both, while Tamburri's (1991) original and perceptive *To Hyphenate or Not to Hyphenate?* examines the hyphen from a political, social, and philosophical perspective. Also, see Tamburri's (1998) other equally suggestive essay "Rethinking Italian/American Studies: From the Hyphen to the Slash and Beyond."

> 1. Not strictly literary autobiographical and memorial texts, whose collection and systematic analysis is, nonetheless, important for a dialectical understanding of the various components of literary history.
> 2. Novels or short stories written in English by members of the Italo-American community, containing predominance of themes that can be considered characteristic of such a community.
> 3. Works by those that I have called writers between two worlds: the Italian expatriates in the United States who write exclusively or largely in Italian. (273)[2]

Valesio's model offers an excellent starting point in trying to navigate both the intricacies of Italian American culture and a literature born out of mixed cultural and linguistic referents.

For this essay, I would like to consider Valesio's third distinction, authors whom he calls "writers between two worlds," in particular two writers I consider exemplary to this category: Giovanni Cecchetti and Joseph Tusiani. Cecchetti and Tusiani, like other writers

---

[2] It is important to note that Valesio "refers to himself and other immigrant authors like him as 'expatriates.'" Ruberto and Sciorra (2017, 5) state that "the half-million or so Italians who immigrated to the United States between 1945 and 1973 can be classified as either working-class or elite." They cite Pasquale Verdicchio who writes that "to this day, professionals who have lived outside of Italy for decades have difficulty defining themselves as emigrants/immigrants."

with similar experiences, operate in and from a reality that is "bilingual, bicultural [and] biconceptual" (Hicks 1989, xxv). In Roland Barthes's terms their artistic perceptions are illuminated from two or more sets of referential codes. "Juxtaposed between multiple cultures" (Hicks 1989, xxiii), these poets create literature that explores, is influenced by, and is sensitive to the different cultural and linguistic referents that help mold it. They are "cultural border writers" (Hicks 1989, xxv).[3]

Giovanni Cecchetti, born in the town of Pescia (Pistoia province) in Tuscany, emigrated to the United States in 1948 and, while developing his poetic voice, went on to become a scholar of Italian letters at various U.S. universities. Those who knew Cecchetti know how much he loved his adopted land, but he at the same time was always and unmistakably Italian, more precisely Tuscan, in his way of being and showing himself to others, often rude but always direct (see note 3). Cecchetti always composed in Italian, be it poetry or prose, not because of a lack of skill and mastery of the English language—a quick cursus through his critical studies written in English instantly dismisses such a notion—but because of an unwavering loyalty and devotion to the culture of Italy and a belief that the only true poetry one can write is done in one's native language. In a

---
[3] See Carravetta's (1994) insightful review essay.

short essay that appeared in *Forum Italicum,* "Sullo scriver poesia," Cecchetti (1992) writes the following:

> E la lingua? È quella in cui si è nati; è la lingua d'un'infanzia trasfigurata, carica di quei sensi che allora sarebbero stati irragiungibili. Nessuno può scrivere poesia in un'altra lingua, sovrapposta e quindi fittizia, che non gli può diventare linguaggio, sebbene ci stia dentro quotidianamente. In questa può scrivere versi, magari dei buoni versi, ma non poesia—la quale non può nascere in chi si trova bloccato nella prigione dell'artificio. Noi che abbiamo avuto un'infanzia in Italia (quell'infanzia che in certo modo include anche l'adolescenza) possiamo scrivere poesia solo in italiano. L'inglese è la lingua della prosa. (251–252)

> (And the language? It is the one in which you are born; it is the language of a transfigured childhood, loaded with those senses that would then have been unattainable. No one can write poetry in another language, superimposed and therefore fictitious, which cannot become a language, even though he is in it every day. In this he can write verses, maybe good verses, but not poetry—which cannot be born in those who find themselves stuck in the prison of artifice. We who had a childhood in Italy [that childhood that in a certain way also includes adolescence] can write poetry only in Italian. English is the language of prose.[4])

---

[4] See Papini's (2007) review of the 2005 translation by Roberta L. Payne of Cecchetti's (1967) *Diario nomade.* All translations are mine.

Cecchetti made his debut in print in 1967 with the poems of *Diario nomade,* and his second collection of poetry, *Impossibile scendere,* appeared in 1978. Fredi Chiappelli, in his 1975 essay "Sulla poesia di Cecchetti," published in *Forum Italicum,* identified exile, memory, the inexorable passage of time, and modern man's existential and spiritual battle among alienated and alienating landscapes and phenomena as the salient thematic elements in Cecchetti's work.

When one considers Cecchetti's (1985) last work of prose, *Danza nel deserto,* the thematic elements identified in his first two volumes of poetry and that Rebecca West put in perspective in her review of *Nel cammino dei monti* (Cecchetti's third collection of poems) are still present and reinforced by his use of the desolate landscape of the California desert as stage and frame for the twelve short stories that comprise this 127-page volume. Cecchetti lived on the margins of the California desert for over forty years. The stories of *Danza nel deserto,*[5] while echoing Dino Buzzati's *Il deserto dei tartari* (1997), strongly reflect Cecchetti's experiences of living and working on the periphery of that American desert landscape for a good part of his life. The desert for Cecchetti is a metaphor for the solitude that envelops humanity in contemporary society

---

[5] The short stories of *Danza nel deserto* are: "Danza nel deserto," "Il telefono," "Il molo," "Il viale dei pirati," "La baia secca," "Le lettere," "Gl'ingessati," "Il castello," "Gl'ingabbiati," "Il cassone," "La macchina dell'aria," and "L'ascensore."

and the squalor that solitude represents. In the desert, nature breaks the boundaries that we consider "normal," that is, livable. With the desert as stage and frame, these stories acquire a highly surrealistic quality; they portray a world of fantasy where reality is in constant flux and transfiguration while at the same time remaining real. As he stated in an interview with Michael Lettieri (1989), the stories are nothing more than "immagini del mondo in cui viviamo, quasi forme simboliche, ossia forme quasi allegoriche" (123) (images of the world in which we live, almost symbolic forms, rather, almost allegorical).

The men and women who populate the world of *Danza nel deserto* are individuals who live in solitude, and the more they try to break the wall of solitude, the stronger and more impenetrable that wall becomes. *Danza nel deserto* is a book about *communication* or, better yet, the *lack of communication* in contemporary society:

> È il mondo in cui vivo ancora: un mondo di gente che ride e che piange di là dalle vetrate, che muove serissima le labbra, senza che non ci sia mai un interlocutore. So che tutti cercano parole, dimentichi del nido del grillo canterino, e poi si contentano della risata solitaria o del sussurro di colomba. (Lettieri 1989, 123)
>
> (It is the world in which I still live: a world of people who laugh and cry from windows, who move their lips very seriously, without an interlocutor. I know

everyone is looking for words, forget the nest of the singing cricket, and then they're content with a solitary laugh or the whisper of a dove.)

In the story "Il telefono," the traveler/narrator of *Danza nel deserto* visits an old school chum who lives in a small one-room house away from civilization. Inside the small house the traveler sees statues of men and women that are really telephones:

> "Non capisco niente," dissi. M'avvicinai a un uomo con gli occhi tesi.
> "Non codesto. È un ventriloquo. Ha il telefono in pancia; ripete solo quel che dicono i vicini." ....
> "Prova a parlare con qualcuno," disse; "Forse risponde ... questo."
> M'avvicinai e dissi nel ricevitore: "Come sta?" Mi giunse una risposta monosillabica, un suono agglutinato, come in cinese.
> Provai le altre statue; le risposte non cambiarono. A volte i suoni scivolavan via; a volte si gonfiavano in modo da sembrar grida disarticolate da giungla. M'arresi.
> "Senti," disse il vecchio compagno di scuola. "Credevo che con un estraneo diventassero normali. Invece ... da principio cominciarono a farmi degli scherzi. Se dicevo qualcosa in un ricevitore, rispondevan con lunghi discorsi in coreano, in persiano, in armeno ... o almeno così credevo, perché spesso non riuscivo nemmeno a riconoscer la lingua.... Pensai che si fossero abituati a questi scherzi perché li avevo collegati alle linee internazionali. Allora li misi sulla rete nazionale. Peg-

gio che peggio: colpi di tosse, abbai, grida, addirittura canzoncine a bocca chiusa. Insomma voci, non parole.... C'è da disperarsi." (Cecchetti 1985, 30–31)

("I don't understand anything," I said. I approached a man with tense eyes.
"Not that one. It's a ventriloquist. He has the phone in his belly; he just repeats what his neighbors say.
"Try talking to someone," he said. "Maybe he'll answer ... this one."
I approached and said into the receiver, "How are you?" I got a monosyllabic answer, an agglutinated sound, as in Chinese.
I tried the other statues; the answers were always the same. Sometimes sounds slipped away; sometimes they swelled up to sound like disarticulated cries from the jungle. I gave up.
"Listen," said the old schoolmate. "I thought they became normal with a stranger. Instead ... from the beginning they started playing jokes on me. If I said anything in a receiver, they would respond with long speeches in Korean, Persian, Armenian ... or so I thought, because I often couldn't recognize the language.... I thought they got used to these jokes because I connected them to international lines. So I connected them to the national network. It was worse than before: coughing, barking, shouting, even closed-mouthed songs. You know, voices not words.... It's enough to drive you mad.")

The protagonists of *Danza nel deserto* attempt communication but are constantly frustrated, either by their own actions or by events that are outside of their sphere of control. They live as in a dream world. Their need to communicate is so intense that they invent ways of communication that are doomed to failure. Why, then, in this world of instant connectivity through technology, is communication so difficult? Cecchetti offers an answer in the above-mentioned interview with Michael Lettieri:

> Il mondo che sognano, quello in cui poi finiscono per vivere, a volte è molto insolito, come è sempre il caso dei sogni; e quindi non è percepibile dagli altri. È percepibile solo da loro stessi, perché gli altri hanno un loro mondo di sogni che è totalmente diverso. Questo spiega perché la comunicazione è così difficile, anzi direi impossibile. E lo è naturalmente non solo per queste persone, ma per tutti gli altri che io non considero. (Lettieri 1989, 125)
>
> (The world they dream of, the one they end up living in, is sometimes very unusual, as is always the case with dreams; and, therefore, it is not perceptible to others. It is understandable only to themselves, because others have their own world of dreams that is totally different. This explains why communication is so difficult, indeed I would say impossible. And it is of course not only for these people, but for everyone else that I don't consider.)

The theme of the "impossibility of communication"

(Lettieri 1989, 126) is one that ties a number of Cecchetti's works together. In *Il villaggio degli inutili*, a collection of stories written when the author was a young man but published in 1981, the initial story, "La sporta del viandante," clearly explores the themes of the impossibility of communication among men/women and of the continuous flux of reality:

> Ogni tanto aprivo la sporta e ne tiravo fuori una casa o dei brandelli, e mi mettevo a studiarmeli in mano. Non mi ci volle molto ad accorgermi che nella sporta avevo creduto di metter l'infinito, ed invece non avevo depositato altro che una gran quantità di limiti. Continuai lo stesso a raccogliere e conservare. ...
> Però troppe eran le cose che avevo e che dovevo portarmi dietro. Un giorno cominciai a tirar fuori quel che ci avevo messo. Ma tutto era incredibilmente cambiato. Ciò che era originariamente bianco s'era fatto rosso, e viceversa. Le cose azzurre eran diventate grigie. Ma che c'era dentro quella sporta per causare simili trasformazioni? Non l'ho mai saputo.
> (Cecchetti 1981a, 17–18)

(Every now and then I would open my bag and pull out a house and some rags, and I'd begin to study them. I believed I was putting a universe of things in my bag, but it didn't take long for me to realize that instead I deposited nothing but a great quantity of limitations. Nonetheless, I kept collecting and storing....

But I had too many things to carry with me. One day I started to take out what I had put into it, but everything had changed incredibly. What was originally white was now red, and vice versa. The blue things had turned gray. What was in that bag that caused such transformations? I never knew.)

The American desert returns as a protagonist in the collection of poems *Nel cammino dei monti*. In the poem titled "Las Vegas," Cecchetti takes the reader to that most surrealistic of experiences: Las Vegas, the city of metal, neon, and glass that rises, like a phoenix, out of the Nevada desert—the city where America dreams and plays. When the poet is faced with this surrealistic sight his agony over the faith of society overwhelms him. Las Vegas is a metaphor for contemporary society, a society that has no foundation, a society built on sand:

> Se si stacca una scaglia ecco che crolla
> a briciole la rete, e non c'è più nemmeno
> un'ampolla opaca al chiodo
>   della parete. (Cecchetti 1980, 43)

> (If a scale breaks off, the net
> collapses into bits, and there isn't even
> an opaque ampoule attached to the nail
>   on the wall.)

Thus, the desert becomes metaphor for contemporary life and society, for an emptiness that is within us and that we are not able to fill. Contemporary American society, in its endless quest for happiness and material success, is destined to fail, and all it can hope for, according to Cecchetti, is the infertile, arid desert.

Cecchetti's intimate ties with Italy and the American West make him a most original multifaceted poetic voice of Italian literature in America. His cultural border crossings produce a literature that captures "both the concrete and the ephemeral nature of the seen world and of lived experience and concentrates on the struggle of human consciousness to move beyond space and time into an acceptance of the limits of both that might lead to the repatriation of the exiled soul" (West 1981, 98).

&

Joseph Tusiani, born more than ninety years ago in the town of San Marco in Lamis (Foggia province), Apulia, is the migrant who came to the United States in 1947 at the age of twenty-three, with a university degree in hand, in search of his father, the father who had emigrated when Tusiani's mother was pregnant with him, the father he had never seen.[6] Tusiani be-

---

[6] In the novel *Il deserto dei tartari* (Buzzati [1997]), Giovanni Drogo, a lieutenant, is sent to a distant fortress on the edge of the desert from which an invasion of the Tatars is expected. The invasion does not take place, and the constant training becomes monotonous and without meaning. Many years pass and one day Drogo, now old, becomes ill just as the much-anticipated event happens: The Tatars advance from the desert without him being able to take part in the defense preparations, and Drogo dies, forgotten by all.

came a naturalized U.S. citizen in 1956 and had for more than sixty years been active in the United States as a poet, translator, critic, lecturer, and professor.

With the now relatively famous verses from "Song of the Bicentennial," "Two languages, two lands, perhaps two souls ... /Am I a man or two strange halves of one?" (1978, 7), Tusiani perfectly verbalizes the plight of the migrant. In *Gente Mia and Other Poems* (1978) and in the autobiographical trilogy *La parola difficile* (1988), *La parola nuova* (1991), and *La parola antica* (1992a) (*The Difficult Word, The New Word, and The Ancient Word*), published thirteen years after *Gente Mia*,[7] Tusiani speaks precisely to that initial impact he had, as an Italian intellectual, with the United States. In these works, Tusiani examines the major themes that are associated with immigration: the spiritually and psychologically violent act of division from one's family and native land (which is the first experience of the new immigrant), the dreams of the migrant, the prejudice he encounters, the process of Americanization, the question of language, the alienation and the realization that the new world is not the "land of hospitality" he believed it was.

When the emigrant, after a long and wearisome

---

[7] The first lines of *La parola difficile* (Difficult Word) are " – Nuova York! Nuova York! Avevo compiuto ventitre anni e ancor non conoscevo mio padre, emigrato in America sei mesi prima che io nascessi." (New York! New New York! I was twenty-three years old and I still did not know my father, who migrated to America six months before I was born.)

crossing, disembarked at Ellis Island he was immediately faced with the first major obstacle: a strange language. Tusiani knew, as do most of those born in another country, that the emigration odyssey takes many forms, first and foremost coming to terms with the actual, physical separation from the country of birth and from family and friends. This most evident element of emigration is initially the most traumatic. When the migrant arrives in the new country, the voyage is not finished; other "voyages" must be undertaken in the quest to assimilate into mainstream U.S. culture. The most important of these voyages is the linguistic/cultural one. By necessity he must immediately begin the journey from one language, Italian or one of the many Italian dialects, to another, American English. Once the process has begun, he slowly, imperceptibly really, begins to lose his native language and the ideas and cultural values that the native language transmits. A cultural transformation begins to take place, and he starts to lose a part of himself. The question of language, or rather loss of language, is of primary importance to Tusiani when discussing the experience of emigration. He introduces this line of reasoning in "Song of the Bicentennial," the first composition of *Gente Mia*, by a series of questions:

> Do I regret my origins by speaking
> this language I acquired? Do I renounce,

by talking now in terms of only dreams,
the *sogni* of my childhood? What has changed
that I had thought unchangeable in me?

(Tusiani 1978, 5)

Tusiani looks at the language question not only as a sociological problem but also as a spiritual dilemma. The answer to these questions is that something *has* changed and that every phrase, every word uttered in English, separates him a little bit more from his roots:

Now every thought I think, each word I say
detaches me a little more from all
I used to love—

(Tusiani 1978, 7)

For Tusiani when *sogni* becomes *dreams*, *cielo* becomes *sky*, and *mamma* is translated to *mother*, much more transpires than the immigrant's process of Americanization and acculturation. Tusiani, cognizant of the fact that words communicate a plethora of memories, images, and emotions, knew that *cielo* elicits mythicized visions of the old world and that *sky* will only remind the immigrant of the ghetto in the immense concrete jungle he now calls home, and when *mamma* is translated to *mother* much of what was his life begins to disintegrate and will eventually be lost as the immigrant moves farther away from Italy and toward American life and culture:

> Mother, I even wonder if I am
> the child I was, the little child you knew,
> for you did not expect your little son
> to grow apart from all that was your world....
> Yet of a sudden he was taught to say
> "mother" for Mamma, and for cielo "sky."
> That very day, we lost each other. (Tusiani 1978, 5)

Loss of the Italian language (or dialect) is for our poet "a betrayal or denial of his original world—indeed his very origin, his very self" (Tusiani 1982, 153–54).

After many years of writing in English, Tusiani returned to Italian in the autobiographical trilogy, where again he takes up the problem of language. In *La parola antica* (The ancient word), the third volume of the trilogy, he discusses it at length:

> Due lingue. La realtà dello sbarbicamento (uso questo termine per indicare lo sradicamento completo) comporta diversi problemi o traumi, prima di tutto quello di un nuovo linguaggio. Progredendo nell'acquisizione della lingua straniera, si corre il rischio, per ragioni di umana vanità, di ritenere inferiore quella materna? ...
>
> Non si cade in questo pericolo se il fenomeno del bilinguismo lo si considera non come conquista ma come rinnegamento forzato delle proprie origini e di se stessi. Il bilingualismo, cioè, diventa sinonimo di disintegrata unità familiare, per cui una madre non è più in grado di comprendere il proprio figlio. Dal giorno in cui il figlio dice "Mother" per "mamma" e "sky" per

"cielo," fra madre e figlio c'è già una separazione spirituale che lo studioso di linguistica non può catalogare. Se le parole sono suoni articolati che simboleggiano e comunicano un'idea, il termine "mamma", a differenza di "mother," il nuovo termine acquisito, simboleggia e comunica un intero mondo di sentimenti che nessuna espressione straniera può comprendere e rispettare. Abolirlo significa rigettare l'esistenza di una fanciullezza intimamente legata a tutti gli episodi, piccoli e grandi, e a tutte le emozioni, importanti e non importanti, connessi ed ispirati da quell'unica parola. Non assimilazione o americanizzazzione, dunque, ma ambivalenza, un'ambivalenza di pensiero e sentimento, di dubbio e di certezza, di sogno e realtà.[8] (Tusiani 1992a, 143–144)

(Two languages. The reality of eradication [I use this term to indicate complete uprooting] involves several problems or traumas, first of all that of a new language. As we progress in the acquisition of the foreign language, do we run the risk, for reasons of human vanity, of believing that the mother tongue is inferior?

One does not fall into this danger if the phenomenon of bilingualism is seen not as a conquest but as a forced denial of one's origins and of oneself. Bilingualism, that is, becomes synonymous with the disintegration of the family unit, whereby a mother is no longer able to understand her child. From the day the child says "mother" for "Mamma" and "sky" for "cielo," there is already a spiritual separation between mother

---

[8] The trilogy and *Il ritorno* (Tusiani 1992b) signal a return to Italian.

and child that the scholar of linguistics cannot catalogue. If words are articulate sounds that symbolize and communicate an idea, the term "mamma," unlike "mother," the new term acquired, symbolizes and communicates a whole world of feelings that no foreign expression can understand and respect. Abolishing it means rejecting the existence of a childhood intimately linked to all episodes, small and large, and to all emotions, important and not important, connected and inspired by that one word. Neither assimilation or Americanization, therefore, but ambivalence, an ambivalence of thought and feeling, of doubt and certainty, of dream and reality.)

The consequence of this transformation is that the immigrant, by expressing himself/herself in the acquired tongue, translates not only the language but his very soul, and in that process of translation he slowly and unrelentingly begins to change. He now has the language and the culture of two lands: "America and Italy but in what order? Shouldn't we say: Italy and America?" ("America e Italia; in quale ordine, però? Non dovremmo dire: Italia e America?") (Tusiani 1992, 143).[9] Tusiani poses these questions because he believes that the immigrant cannot totally assimilate into the adopted culture:[10]

---

[9] It is important to note that the trilogy is also the biography of Tusiani's family in America and a grand tour of Italian American history as he understands it.
[10] Also see "Song of the Bicentennial" (Tusiani 1978).

Posta in termini diversi la domanda è: fino a qual punto l'emi-grato può assimilare la nuova lingua e la nuova civiltà, e in che maniera dimenticare e rinnegare sé stesso in mezzo alle nuove e impellenti esigenze della sua vita? Anche se la risposta sia priva di validità scientifica, il poeta ci dice che non esiste, e non può esistere, un assorbimento totale, *e che non potrà mai esserci un'accetta-zione totale, cioè spirituale, delle tradizioni della nuova terra.* (Tusiani 1992, 143: emphasis mine)

(In different terms, the question is: to what extent can the emigrant assimilate the new language and the new civilization, and how can he forget and disavow himself in the midst of the new and urgent demands of his life? Even if the answer is devoid of scientific validity, the poet tells us that there can't be, and cannot exist, a total absorption, and *that there can never be a total spiritual acceptance of the traditions of the new land.*)

Tusiani's continuous feeling of uprootedness lies primarily within this context of never having fully "spiritually" assimilated into American culture. He expressed it best in his "Song of the Bicentennial":

Then who will solve this riddle of my day?
Two languages, two lands, perhaps two souls. ...
Am I a man or two strange halves of one?
(Tusiani 1978, 7)

It is precisely the unsolved riddle and the feeling of

being suspended between two worlds, of not belonging, and of navigating between two cultural systems that, I believe, pushes Tusiani to return to Italian, the language of his native land, for his autobiography.[11]

The resolution is his awareness of being suspended between two worlds, his acceptance of his biculturalism, for which, instead of seeing himself as not belonging to either one or the other world, he can accept himself as the man of "two languages, two lands ... two [socio-cultural] souls." After forty years the riddle has been solved. The questions posed in "Song of the Bicentennial" have now become statements (Giordano 1994, 82).

As Paolo Valesio wrote in the introduction to the special issue of *Gradiva*, "Italian Poets in America," "Exile is a slinking beast; it bides its time, without hurry, but it gets you in the end. When all the illusions of moderation and equilibrium and normal routine are gone, we find ourselves face to face with a radical choice" (Valesio 1993, 5). The individual can accept his existential condition as "Other," or he can deny this condition and try to assimilate as much as possible in the new reality and "with a constant policing of all his rebellious thoughts, doubts, or bursts of despair—live out his life as an adoptive existence" (Valesio 1993, 5).

The two poets that I have briefly touched upon

---

[11] For a more complete analysis, see Siani (1999).

confronted their situation in radically different ways. For Cecchetti, the literary journey was different, his creative writing is in Italian; English is the language of his academic work and translation. The intimate ties that he had with Italian culture and with the American West made him one of the original voices of Italian literature in the United States. His continuous drifting back and forth across the border of two cultures gave life to literature that captures both the ephemeral nature of American society and the real concrete nature of a lived experience, concentrated in the effort of human consciousness aimed at pushing beyond space and time toward acceptance of the limits of both.

Tusiani is known as a poet who wrote in four languages[12] and who later in life returned to writing in Italian and his native Gargano dialect to somehow find a solution to his psychological state of being a man divided between two lands and two cultures.[13] But try as he might, all the years living and working

---

[12] Tusiani studied Italian in school and at the university and spoke it when he was not at home, but his native language is the dialect spoken in San Marco in Lamis (Gargano, Apulia). This is his first language, the language that is full of cultural significance; this can be said about most Italians who grew up speaking dialect at home.

[13] The bibliography on Tusiani is vast. For more information on his treatment of the emigration question, see the bibliography of the Fondo Tusiani (Università del Salento, founded and curated by Emilo Bandiera until his retirement, and in particular the studies listed in the Works Cited below. See the Fondo Tusiani for his writings in Latin and dialect.

in the United States had a profound effect on his life and on his work. In the last episode of the *La parola antica* Tusiani recounts that one day, on an airplane returning from a trip to Italy, he dreams that he finds himself with his mother in a long corridor with many doors illuminated by a bright white light. There is a door at each end of the corridor, one marked "Entrance" and the other marked "Exit." Tusiani and his mother begin walking toward the door marked "Exit." When they get to the end of the corridor they realize that now the sign on the door as changed to "Entrance" and that the door at the other end of the corridor says "Exit":

> Arrivai sotto quella scrittura e lessi "Entrata". Mi voltai e vidi, lì dov'era mia madre la parola "Uscita".... Rifeci il cammino, ma quando raggiunsi mia madre, in alto, al posto di «Uscita» lessi nuovamente «Entrata». ... E per quaranta volte, affannato, ansioso, con la speranza e la disperazione che mi spingevano e guidavano, corsi da un'estremità all'altra di quell'enorme corridoio. (Tusiani 1992a, 308)

> (I arrived at the door and the sign read "Entrance." I turned around and saw, where my mother was, the word "Exit." ... I made my way back, but when I reached my mother, at the top, instead of "Exit," I read "Entrance" again. ... Forty times, breathless, anxious, with the hope and despair that drove me, I ran from one end of that enormous corridor to the other.)

In the middle of his dream, Tusiani is awakened by the flight attendant announcing their arrival in New York City. The book ends with this short paragraph:

> Andando verso il Bronx, nella limousine della Poten notai un altro particolare: i tergicristalli, strusciando da destra a sinistra, da sinistra a destra, sembravano dire Entrata-Uscita, Uscita-Entrata, ma non sapevo più che cosa significassero quelle due parole, né a chi fossero rivolte. (Tusiani 1992a, 310)

> (Heading toward the Bronx, in the Poten limousine [his brother's petroleum company], I noticed another detail: the windshield wipers, rubbing from right to left, from left to right, they seemed to say Entrance-Exit, Exit-Entrance, but I didn't know what those two words meant, nor to whom they were addressed.)

A careful reading of the last pages of Tusiani's trilogy suggests that maybe the poet has come to an understanding of his condition as Other, and it is really very simple. In the motion of the windshield wipers that seemed to say to him Entrance-Exit, Exit-Entrance, Tusiani finally realizes that he is a man suspended between two worlds, that he is a man of two languages and two souls.

Bibliogrpahy

Buzzati, Dino. 1997. *Il deserto dei tartari*. Milan: Mondadori.
Carravetta, Peter. 1994. "Review Essay: *Border Writing: The Multidimensional Text*. D. Emily Hicks Minneapolis: Uni-

versity of Minnesota Press, 1991." In *Differentia: Review of Italian Thought*, edited by Peter Carravetta, 6. Stony Brook, NY: Stony Brook University Press.

Cecchetti, Giovanni. 1967. *Diario nomade*. Padua: Rebellato.

Cecchetti, Giovanni. 1981. *Il villaggio degli inutili*. Venice: Rebellato.

Cecchetti, Giovanni. 1980 *Nel cammino dei monti*. Florence: Vallecchi.

Cecchetti, Giovanni. 1985. *Danza nel deserto*. Venice: Rebellato.

Cecchetti, Giovanni. 1992. *Forum Italicun* 26 (May): 251–252.

Chiappelli, Fredi. 1975. "Sulla poesia di Cecchetti." *Forum Italicum* (June/September): 123–130.

Fontanella, Luigi. 2003. *La parola trasfuga. Scrittori Italiani in America*. Fiesole: Cadmo.

Fontanella, Luigi, and Paolo Valesio, eds. 1993. "Italian Poets in America," a special issue, *Gradiva: International Journal of Italian Literature* 5.1, Stony Brook, NY.

Garofalo, Piero, Elizabeth Leake, and Dana Renga. 2019. *Internal Exile in Fascist Italy: History and Representations of confino*. Manchester, UK: Manchester University Press.

Giordano, Paolo A. 1991. "From Southern Italian Emigrant to Reluctant American: Joseph Tusiani's *Gente Mia* and Other *Poems*, in *From the Margin: Writings in Italian Americana*, edited by Anthony J. Tamburri, Paolo A. Giordano, and Fred L. Gardaphé, 314–326. West Lafayette, IN: Purdue University Press.

Giordano, Paul, ed. 1994. *Joseph Tusiani Poet Translator Humanist: An International Homage*. New York: Bordighera.

Hicks, D. Emily. 1989. *Border Writing: The Multidimensional Text*. Minneapolis: University of Minnesota Press.

Lettieri, Michael. 1989. "Danza nel deserto: intervista a Giovanni Cecchetti." *Ipotesi* 80 (June): 123–130.

Marazzi, Martino. 2011. *A occhi aperti. Letteratura dell'emigrazione e mito americano*. Milan: Franco Angeli.

Papini, Maria Carla. 2007. "Review of Giovanni Cecchetti. *Nomad diary* (Diario nomade)," *Italica* 84.2/3: 651–53.

Perez-Firmat, Gustavo. 1994. *Life on the Hyphen: The Cuban-American Way*.

Petrillo, Raymond, ed. 1997. *Contrappunti / Counterpoints: Selected Prose of Giovanni Cecchetti*. New York: Peter Lang, International Academic.

Ruberto, Laura, and Joseph Sciorra, eds. 2017. *New Italian Migrations in the United States: Art and Culture Since 1945*, Vol. 2. Champaign-Urbana: University of Minnesota Press

Siani, Cosma. 1999. *L'io diviso. Joseph Tusiani fra emigrazione e letteratura*. Rome: Cofine.

Siani, Cosma. 2000. *Two Languages, Two Lands. L'opera letteraria di Joseph Tusiani*. San Marco in Lamis: Quaderni del Sud.

Tamburri, Anthony Julian. 1991. *To Hyphenate or Not to Hyphenate? The Italian/American Writer: An Other American*. Toronto: Guernica.

Tamburri, Anthony Julian. 1998. "Rethinking Italian/American Studies: From the Hyphen to the Slash and Beyond." In *Beyond the Margin: Readings in Italian Americana*, edited by Paolo Giordano and Anthony Julian Tamburri, 243–283. Madison-Teaneck, NJ: Farleigh Dickinson University Press.

Tamburri, Anthony Julian. 2016. "Un rimpatrio linguistico, ovvero un recupero culturale? Il ritorno di Joseph Tusiani." *Italica* 92(2): 338–356.

Tusiani, Joseph. 1978. *Gente mia and Other Poems*. Stone Park, IL: Italian Cultural Center.

Tusiani, Joseph. 1982. "The Themes of Deracination and Americanization in *Gente Mia and Other Poems*." *Ethnic Groups* 4: 149–176.

Tusiani, Joseph. 1988. *La parola difficile: autobiografia di un Italo-Americano*. Bari: Schena.

Tusiani, Joseph. 1991. *La parola nuova autobiografia di un Italo-Americano*. Bari: Schena.

Tusiani, Joseph. 1992a. *La parola antica: autobiografia di un Italo-Americano*. Bari: Schena.

Tusiani, Joseph. 1992b. *Il ritorno*. Bari: Schena.

Valesio, Paolo. 1989. "Writer between Two Worlds: Italian Writing in the United States Today." *Differentia* 3–4 (Spring/Autumn): 259–276.

Valesio, Paolo. 1993. Introduction. "Italian Poets in America," Luigi Fontanella and Paolo Valesio, eds. *Gradiva* 5.1: 5–8.

Valesio, Paolo, and Peter Carravetta, eds. 1993. *Poesaggio*. Quinto di Treviso: Pagus.

Viscusi, Robert. 1981. "*De vulgari eloquentia*: An Approach to the Language of Italian American Fiction." *Yale Italian Studies* I.3: 21–38.

West, Rebecca. 1981. Review of Cecchetti's *Cammino dei monti* (Firenze: Vallecchi, 1980). *Forum Italicum*.

Forced Emigration:
Between Autobiography and Romance

Everyone has seen and recalls the moving and tragic images of the great groups of Italian emigrants, especially from the South, who, between 1880 and 1924, made the exhausting passage on overloaded ships and in poor conditions, sustained by the mirage of America, that mythical "New World" full of hope and expectation.

Many know by now of the sociological effects of that enormous and unprecedented phenomenon: of human-social upheaval, of customs and traditions, of mobility and encounter — a clash between human masses of different backgrounds and histories — of cultural formation, with the outcomes either of leveling in the "melting pot" or else of racial and cultural particularization. Not everyone knows, however, about the more specifically cultural and psychological effects of estrangement and wearying re-creation, of confusion and the multiplication of identities. And of more besides.

Emigration from Italy to America has reached extraordinarily high numbers of people, and much has been written about it by historians, sociologists, Anthropologists, etc., but it is interesting that a fact so true, so dramatic, and of such long duration has not found a response equal to its importance in the Italian narrative. The great Italian emigration of the nineteenth and twentieth centuries lacked its great writer. In America there is a rich narrative tradition. Since the end of the last century, emigrants and children of emigrants have written a significant number of novels and autobiographies, which, apart from the few exceptions such as Pietro di Donato's *Christ in Concrete* and Mario Puzo's *The Fortunate Pilgrim* and *The Godfather*, have received little attention from either literary critics or the reading public. It is noteworthy that *The Godfather* has become the quintessential bestseller; unfortunately, this supremacy is due to a misguided reason: the special interest and attraction that America has always harbored for the myth of the Mafia.

Until a few years ago, critical interest in this literature has been negligible. Literature chronicling emigration and the lives of the emigrant and his descendants in the United States has always been a literature without a home: It was not recognized by the American family of letters, and Italianists in the various American universities, at least those who knew such a body of literature existed, almost always relegated it to the margins as a form of writing without literary value, dismissing it as "sociology." In the past twenty-five years much has changed, mainly because of the advent of "cultural studies" and "new historicism." Lately in the United States multiculturalism and ethnic literature are in vogue. In the wake of this, the interest in Italian American culture and literature has finally emerged from its narrow niche and is finding its way into university departments of English and Italian and into various literary conferences. Among the most important studies published so far it is worth mentioning Rose Basile-Green's *The Italian-American Novel: A Document of the Interaction of Two Cultures*; Robert Viscusi's "*De vulgari eloquentia*: An Approach to the Language of Italian American Fiction"; William Boelhower's three studies "The Immigrant Novel as Genre," *Immigrant Autobiography in the United States,* and *Through a Glass Darkly: Ethnic Semiosis*; Helen Barolini's *The Dream Book: An Anthology of Writing by Italian American Women*; Paolo Valesio, "Writer Between Two Worlds: Italian Writing in the United States Today"; Anthony Julian Tamburri's *From the Margin: Writings in Italian Americana* and *To Hyphenate or Not to Hyphenate: The Italian-American Writer An Other American*; Fred Gardaphé's "My House Is Not Your House: Jerre Mangione and Italian-American Autobiography," *La letteratura dell'emigrazione. Scrittori di lingua italiana nel mondo,* and *Italian Signs American Streets: The Evolution of Italian American Narrative*. Also of note are journals such as *Italian Americana, la bella figura,* and *VIA: Voices in Italian Americana* and the double issue of *Differentia*, devoted entirely to the critical study of Italian American literature.[1]

---

[1] Prior to Rose Basile Green's historical study, it was rare for critics to address the writing of Italian Americans. One of the earliest acts of criticism came from Jerre Mangione, who in 1935 wrote a review of Garibaldi Lapolla's novel *The Grand Gennaro* in the *New Republic*. In this review,

It is important to dwell briefly on two of the publications mentioned above because of their seminal importance in the development and recognition of this literature. The first is Basile Green's *The Italian-American Novel: A Document of the Interaction of Two Cultures* (Fairleigh Dickinson UP, 1974), a landmark book for being the first to attempt a theory of Italian American fiction. In this study, Basile Green, creating a sociological paradigm, divides Italian American literary production into five stages: (1) impact with the new culture, (2) desire of the immigrant to immerse himself in the new culture and become "American," (3) repulsion at or reaction against the culture of the ancestors and attempt to identify with the "American" culture, in which only non-Italian American themes are treated, (4) return to the old Italian American themes, and (5) the Italian American writer's sense of affinity with the American culture. In addition to providing us with an early codification of Italian American literature, with this volume Basile Green offers the first comprehensive bibliography of Italian American literature and culture.

The second pivotal moment in the development of the study of this literary phenomenon was the publica-

---

Mangione introduced the reader of this important magazine to the rarity of the Italian American character in an English-language literary work and credited Lapolla with creating "Italian-Americans who are vivid and alive, probably a novelty to the ordinary person who, not knowing them intimately, was likely to form an opinion of them (Italian Americans) through mob movies" (Review 313).

tion of the book *Italian Signs American Streets*. In this book Gardaphé, re-addressing the Viconian concept of history, approaches the reading of Italian American fiction from the perspective of ethnic studies. He begins his historical reading with texts drawn from the oral tradition, mostly autobiographies, and traces the development of this narrative through the most well-known writers, including di Donato, Fante, Mangione, and Puzo, continuing through the reinvention of ethnicity with Helen Barolini's *Umbertina*, Tina De Rosa's *Paper Fish*, and *Ghost Dance*, by Carol Maso. The discussion eventually reaches the postmodern era, where the works of Don DeLillo, Gilbert Sorrentino, and Mary Caponegro are examined, works that are no longer specifically ethnic but are always imbued with what Gardaphé identifies as *Italianità*.

On Italian American literature and its various aspects, Paolo Valesio, in his article "The Writer Between Two Worlds: Italian Writing in the United States Today," which appeared in *Differentia*, writes:

> It is important to keep in mind a saying from medieval scholasticism: *Distingue frequenter*. Confusing codes, registers and genres (literary or cultural) often leads to mutual misunderstanding. In the case of mixed communities such as Italian-American, Hispanic-American, African-American, etc., the risk is even greater.... It then becomes necessary to distinguish between the following:

1. Autobiographies that are not strictly literary, and memoirs—the collection and systematic analysis of which are nevertheless important for a dialectic knowledge of the various components of literary history.
2. Novels or stories written in English by members of the Italian American community, predominantly based on themes that can be considered characteristic of this community.
3. Literary works by those I have called writers between two worlds: Italian expatriates in the United States who write exclusively or mostly in Italian. (273)

Valesio's model offers an excellent starting point for the student who wants to enter the labyrinth of a culture and literature born from multicultural and multilingual references.

Using this model as a guide, I would like to talk briefly about some books that I see as examples of these three categories, in order: *Son of Italy*, by Pascal D'Angelo, the autobiography of an emigrant who wants to tell his story; *Olives on the Apple Tree*, by Guido D'Agostino, and *Umbertina*, by Helen Barolini, novels that deal with Italian American themes and highlight generational conflicts; and the autobiographical trilogy *La parola difficile*, *La parola nuova*, and *La parola antica*, by Joseph Tusiani, a writer for whom I would use Valesio's label of "a writer between two worlds."

In 1924 Pascal D'Angelo published his autobiography *Son of Italy*, in which we follow the story of an emigrant who from an illiterate laborer transforms himself, reinventing himself as a poet in the English language and competing for a poetry prize sponsored by The Nation magazine. In this book, D'Angelo draws on the Dante of *Vita Nuova* in the mixture of prose and poetry and in the functional relationship between the two. But unlike *Vita Nuova*, where the architecture of the work consists of a wide selection of poems linked together by passages of prose that have an explanatory function, D'Angelo inserts only eight complete poems into his autobiographical 185-page prose text. Furthermore, while "truth" for D'Angelo can be expressed only through poetry, the function of prose is to create the context in which this truth is pronounced and takes on value; it is not an explanation or paraphrase of the poetic text.

Son of Italy is the story of a journey not only physical but also spiritual that begins in the mountains of Abruzzo (the first five chapters take place in Italy) and ends in New York. It is a journey that begins in a primordial world where "night and darkness remind us that man does not control, nor can he control, his environment" (Gardaphé 41) and where everything seems reduced to a dream, and it ends in a modern world where the metaphors of D'Angelo's poetry shift from the peasant realm of nature to the realm of the city.

This uprooting takes D'Angelo from a place in which man, nature, and "heaven" act, for the most part, in harmony with the other to an America where man does not live in harmony with the environment but seems to be continually fighting with it. This lack of harmony creates tensions that often result in confusion for the protagonist, confusion aggravated by the language problem that sometimes creates comic situations. When D'Angelo reads the street signs for the first time, he is amazed and writes:

> I began to notice that there were signs at the corners of the streets with "Ave.! Ave!" How religious a place this must be that expresses its devotion at every at every crossing, I mused. Still, they did not put the "Ave" before the holy word as in "Ave Maria" but rather after. How topsy turvy. (61)

Other times, language problems put him in awkward situations. After having a fight with a coworker, he realizes he has a large bruise under one eye. Mortified, and wanting to hide the fact that this bruise is the result of a punch, he has someone teach him the phrase "fall down":

> First I asked the foreman what the English for falling down was. He told me, "faw don."
> I began to repeat to myself, "faw don, faw don ...."
> It was evening and I was picking my way down an icy road toward the town. Right outside the first houses

> two American fellows were quarreling, and I paused to watch and listen. One of them was shaking his fist under the other man's nose and saying, "You damn!"
>
> Somehow, I forgot "faw don" and as I walked away I was repeating "You damn! You damn! ... " Unconscious of the change.
>
> The first man I met was an American brakeman, who wore a collar on Sunday and whose acquaintance I esteemed greatly.
>
> He greeted me, "Hello, Pat!" Everybody called me Pat. "What's happened to you?"
>
> "Me?" And I assumed an expression of sad innocence. "Me? You damn!" and I pointed to the ground.
>
> "What?" he explained.
>
> "Yes," I repeated in a louder voice, "You damn! You damn!"
>
> He laughed, said something and walked on, leaving me a little offended and grieved at his lack of sympathy.
>
> The same thing happened when I met a young lady who worked in the yard office. And all around the place I went repeating my sad tale of "You damn!" When finally, one man made me understand what I had been saying, I was so ashamed that I hurried straight home. (73)

In his book it's clear that D'Angelo is speaking to us from the periphery—both literary and socio-cultural—of America, his adopted country. And he's so deeply in the margins that in order to be published and have credibility, the book had to be presented by an influential critic of American culture, Carl Van Doren, editor of the monthly cultural and political magazine *The Nation*. In *Son of Italy*, D'Angelo reaffirms the immigrant's creed that America is the land of hope and opportunity, and he does this while maintaining his own ethnic marginality and not assuming the central position of the assimilated immigrant. He chooses the voice of the periphery, the voice of the figure on the margins. As Boelhower writes, D'Angelo "is an Italian-American Prometheus" who wrests control of his destiny from the primordial gods of the mountains of his native Abruzzo and holds it tightly in his hands. The last part of *Son of Italy* is modeled on the cultural code of the "self-made man," a concept that is at the heart of the American myth. The difference is that D'Angelo, instead of choosing money as a symbol and measure of success, he chose poetry and thus radically distanced himself from the immigrant's credo.[2]

Published in 1940, Guido Dagostino's novel *Olives on the Apple Tree* addresses via the two faces of America—the America of promises and the America of broken promises—generational conflicts and the issue of assimilation.

Federico and Giustina Gardella are two immigrants who have achieved what they consider to be the American dream: ownership of three factories. They pay dearly for this success: loss of their ethnic identity and the destruction of the family.

---

[2] See Boelhower (1982, 97–135) and Gardaphé (37–47).

Giustina Gardella found it a great satisfaction to live in the village and have her own home situated where she could pause in her housework and glimpse the shabby life up on the hill from which she saved her own family. For it was Giustina who decided, when the family first moved into the neighborhood, that they were not going to live with the poor Italian on Wop-Roost, but right down in the center of things where there was a chance to take advantage of the opportunity of the New World. (1)

The Gardellas have two children, Emilio and Elena, who were born in the new world. Elena remains faithful to the family ideals and after attending university returns home and works in the family business. She lives a monotonous and resigned life. Emilio, on the other hand, rebels and tries to annul his ethnic identity. The "American" son of Federico and Giustina, who becomes a doctor, even goes so far as to change his name from Emilio to Emile, and, so as not to be recognized as Italian, wants also to anglicize his surname from Gardella to Gardell: "At the hospital everybody gets into the habit of calling you by your last name. Hey Gardella, they say. Makes me feel like a wop greenhorn." (33). He doesn't want to be associated with the "wops," he doesn't want them as patients, and he certainly doesn't want to marry one: "Marrying a wop! I could commit suicide as far as my profession goes" (221). For Emile it's important to be in the company of respectable people (that is, people with money) and to have an Anglo-Saxon girlfriend. Emile speaks like them and dresses like them. In his rush to assimilation and his anxiety to deny his ethnicity, Emile fails, however, to correctly read the signs of the culture whose acceptance he seeks. He believes that this is a society that only values money and success. Emile doesn't realize that this culture, even if different from the Italian one of his parents, is not only based on money and success but has its own code of values: a code that, as I say, he can't understand. This mistake will ruin him, and by the end of the novel Emile will find himself rejected by everyone: by his family and the culture that he had disowned, and by the "American" society that had such a strong attraction for him.

D'Agostino juxtaposes the character of Emilio with that of Marco, a tramp who arrives in the village one evening in the summer. Marco, a tramp not by choice but by necessity, sees America and the American experience in a radically different way. Endowed with greater sensitivity, he perceives the danger inherent in renouncing ethnic identity and in the attempt to assimilate too quickly into American culture. Marco is disappointed by America and by the Italians who have accepted the American myth and dream without ever questioning the absolute positivity of the experience:

> I see one big country — rich, beautiful, like never I have seen before and all I feel is I want to keep moving.

> Everybody I find like your doctor here, and Nick—mad sore like hell about something. Nobody satisfied with anything, and I have become so sick with this American sickness ....
>
> And that is America.... Everything is all mixed up. The farmer is no longer a farmer, he has become a businessman. The man who was good at handling stone now is a slave in the laundry. It's no longer work but money that makes one man different from the other. I look for the Italians. What did I find? No longer an Italian but a bastard Italian. He immediately forgets everything from the old country and becomes just like the Americans he is working for. But he does not become American and he is no longer Italian. Something in the middle—no good for himself and no good for the country. A real *bastardo*! (26–28)

After analyzing the problem of the loss of ethnic identity, Marco offers a solution:

> Marco picked up an olive. He munched it and nodded his head. "The olive that jumps to the apple tree. The olive that shouts that it is an apple. There is the mistake. There is the whole trouble.... I have said it many times and I will say it many times more. Easy. Easy. The worry of the immigrant is not being an American. The worry is to work, to produce what you can produce and that is what makes you an American." (295)

With an ending not entirely unexpected, we see that while Emilio has ruined himself, Marco reaps the benefits of his ethnic sensitivity: He is accepted by the

Gardella family, at least by Federico and Elena, with whom he has fallen in love, and he receives the inheritance that was to be Emilio's.

&

Helen Barolini's novel *Umbertina*, originally published by Seaview Press in 1979, tells the story of three generations of the Longobardi family.³ These generations and their values are represented by the three protagonists: Umbertina, the young shepherdess who emigrates from Calabria; Marguerite, Umbertina's granddaughter; and Tina, Marguerite's daughter. Each of these women represents a period of development in the process of assimilation from Italian to American culture. *Umbertina*, however, differs from most Italian American novels because the author changes the gender of the main characters; he becomes she.⁴ As Barolini develops the theme of ethnic identity, she is also dealing with the identity of the woman who must fight

---

³ For this essay I have followed the 1999 edition of the novel published by Feminist Press. After I published the Italian version of this essay, two essays later appeared on Umbertina, of which I would like to mention here: Edvige Giunta's "Blending 'Literary' Discourses: Helen Barolini's Italian/American Narratives" and Maria Kotsaftis's "A Female Odyssey in Quest of the Self."

⁴ In her afterword to the 1999 edition, Edvige Giunta states: "An epic feminist narrative, Barolini's first novel offers almost a textbook case of immigrant history, as experienced by the women of a family that moves from the absolute poverty of peasantry to the oppression of being immigrant and working class to the material comfort of middle-class life but remains haunted by the shadows of the past" (427).

to realize herself in a patriarchal society.⁵ Furthermore, this novel stands out from the others because Barolini places the phenomenon of emigration at the heart of the unification of Italy. This becomes a felicitous choice because in this way she clearly indicates that the process of unification was one of the fundamental factors in the phenomenon of mass emigration:

> It was a new thing to be Italian and the men said it brought new troubles: Taxes had come on salt and even flour milling, so the poor could no longer afford their daily bread, and many of the younger ones had gone up into the mountains, even as far as Aspromonte, to live as bandits rather than be conscripted into the armies of the new nations. There were shepherds, too ... who had lost out when some of the old estates that had allowed pasturage on communal lands were broken up and the new money that bought them closed them off. (28)

Like *Olives on the Apple Tree*, *Umbertina* tells the story of the conflicts of an Italian American family across four generations. Lopreato, instead of calling the emigrant generation "first generation," labels it "peasant."⁶ The first generation is represented by Umbertina, a shepherdess from a small village in the Calabrian mountains, who marries Serafino, much older than her, not for love but for convenience. Unable to create a life and a future for herself in Italy, the family

---

⁵ See Tamburri (1991a) and Giunta (1999).
⁶ See Campisi and Lopreato in this regard.

decides to emigrate to the United States: The idea is Umbertina's. In America, Umbertina and Serafino achieve the American dream of a business that brings great profit to the family and allows them to buy the most beautiful house in the area. All this is due to the tenacity and shrewdness of Umbertina, who nonetheless must submit to the will of a social system where the father is considered the head of the family and the sons have more freedom than the daughters: at the entrance of the company, for example, one reads, "Longobardi and Sons."

In the novel, Barolini doesn't dwell much on the second generation, that of Marguerite's parents. When she does talk about them, she paints a picture of people who see everything from an economic point of view and who try to erase their origins by proclaiming themselves American instead of Italian:

> Marguerite learned that it was not nice to look too Italian and to speak bad English the way Uncle Nunzio did. Italians were not serious people, her father would say — look at Jimmy Durante and Al Capone; Sacco and Vanzetti. Italians were buffoons, anarchists and gangsters, womanizers. "What are we Dad, aren't we Italians?" She would ask. "We're Americans," he'd say firmly. (150)

Typical of the third generation, Marguerite breaks with the old Italian American business and the middle-class values that defined her family: religion and the obsession to "make good" economically:

> Then there was religion. For Marguerite her family's religion was like their fireless fireplaces, without warmth or comfort or honesty. Just show. ...
>
> Talk was always in words of commercial transaction. Children owed parents respect; children paid back what was done for them by studying hard and leading good lives; children had to capitalize on their talents; doings so bore dividends in life; you didn't go around with certain people because there was no profit in it. The family motto could have been "Money Talks." (154)[7]

Marguerite's rebellion takes shape in her choices of lifestyle. Her first attempt to run away from home results in a disastrous marriage that ends in divorce. She later marries an Italian poet, Alberto Morosini, whom she meets during a trip to Italy, and they have a daughter, Tina. Marguerite chooses literature and photography as possible careers.[8]

As the first to break away from a more traditional way of life, as the daughter of parents who renounced their ethnicity and accepted the values of the American middle class, Marguerite finds herself in an unusual position: She must realize her potential as an independent woman and face her ethnicity without positive role models to follow. In contextualizing Marguerite's story

---

[7] See also Tamburri (1991a)
[8] For this aspect of the novel, see Tamburri's *A Semiotic of Ethnicity*, 48–94.

within the novel, we see that her attempts mostly fail and leave her feeling deeply frustrated. Furthermore, she is cognizant of the fact that, like her mother and grandmother, she too is both part of and also a victim of a patriarchal society. Despite her desire for independence, her life is determined by the personality of her husband, against whom she rebels by having extramarital affairs.

After the car accident that kills Marguerite, her life can be summarized by the last two entries in her diary, as Tamburri points out. The first entry reinforces her ethnic dilemma:

> All those snooty, shining, girls. They know who they are and where they're going.... I'm the only Italian name here. They're all saying they're going to be writers or doctors.... Whoever told me I could do any of that? (310)

The final entry in the diary highlights the dilemma of being a woman:

> Is this the bill for happiness? Is this paying the goddamn fiddler? Now I'm pregnant and it's Massimo's child and who else but me is going to pay? Now what? Ask him to leave his wife? [...] A backroom abortion? [...] What could I tell Alberto? What do women do in Italy ... or anyplace? (312)

Born in Italy but raised in America during the sixties, Tina, Marguerite's daughter and the protagonist of the third book in the novel, is part of that generation that gave life to a cultural and sexual revolution that openly challenged the norms keeping women in a subordinate condition. She, like her mother, experiences the conflict of being a person who is part of two worlds and two cultures. A native of Italy, she loves her birth country but understands that if she wants to have a career she must immerse herself in the American system. She chooses an academic life—she studies Italian with the aim of becoming a professor in an American university, earning a living and not having to depend on a man. And as Gardaphé writes, "By choosing academic life, Tina realizes the hopes her mother dreamed of" (128). Having solved the dilemma of oppression, she frees herself to face the ethnic dilemma. Tina resembles her great-grandmother more than her mother:

> Your mother was never happy, married or not.... Your mother, Tina, never knew what she wanted. But you're more like my mother, the Umbertina for whom you were named. She was a strong person, and she stuck to her guns.

Through Umbertina, Marguerite, and Tina, Barolini traces the evolution of Italian American women through the generations in their search for an identity. Umbertina's work and success are never recognized, even though she was the driving force behind the family's fortune; Marguerite died just as she was beginning to realize the possibilities open to her; Tina, using as her models the mythologized story of her grandmother Umbertina, her mother's life, and the academic life she chose, is an accomplished woman, at ease both as a woman and as an Italian American.

&

I would like to finish this essay by focusing on Joseph Tusiani, poet, translator, and author of an autobiographical trilogy: *La parola difficile, La parola nuova,* and *La parola antica,* three books linked by the subtitle "Autobiography of an Italian-American." I conclude with this writer, about whom I have already written many pages and edited a volume of essays, because I believe Tusiani is the last representative of that Italian American culture linked to the era of the great emigration and also strongly underestimated by scholars dealing with this subject.

In his trilogy, Tusiani eloquently and respectfully addresses the phenomenon of Italian emigration to the United States and reflects on one of the most terrifying aspects of the new American reality, the English language.

When the emigrant arrives at Ellis Island after a long, tortuous, and tiring ocean crossing, he soon realizes that the journey is not over and that he must undertake other "journeys" in his quest to assimilate into the dominant, American culture. The most important of these journeys is the linguistic-cultural one. The emigrant must immediately begin the journey from his mother tongue, normally the dialect of his native village, to American English. Once this process has begun, the emigrant, whose social status changes from emigrant to immigrant, begins to lose his native language and the cultural ideas and values that one's language transmits. A cultural transformation takes place during which the emigrant loses a part of himself. The language problem is of primary importance for Tusiani, and he deals with it not only from a sociological point of view but also as a spiritual dilemma.

> Due lingue. La realta dello sbarbicamento (uso questo termine per indicare lo sradicamento completo) comporta diversi problemi o traumi, prima di tutto quello di un nuovo linguaggio. Progredendo nell'acquisizione della lingua straniera, si corre il rischio, per ragioni di umana vanita, di ritenere inferiore quella materna? ...
>
> Non si cade in questo pericolo se il fenomeno del bilinguismo lo si considera non come conquista ma come rinnegamento forzato delle proprie origini e di sé stessi. Il bilinguismo, cioè, diventa sinonimo di disintegrata unita familiare, per cui una madre non é più in grado di comprendere il proprio figlio. Dal giorno in cui il figlio dice "Mother" per "mamma" e "sky" per "cielo," fra madre e figlio c'è già una separazione spirituale che lo studioso di linguistica non può catalogare. Se le parole sono suoni articolati che simboleggiano e comunicano un'idea, il termine "mamma," a differenza di "mother,"

il nuovo termine acquisito, simboleggia e comunica un intero mondo di sentimenti che nessuna espressione straniera può comprendere e rispettare. Abolirlo significa rigettare l'esistenza di una fanciullezza intimamente legata a tutti gli episodi, piccoli e grandi, e a tutte le emozioni, importanti e non importanti, connessi ed ispirati da quell'unica parola. Non assimilazione o americanizzazione, dunque, ma ambivalenza, un'ambi-valenza di pensiero e sentimento, di dubbio e di certezza, di sogno e realtà (*La parola antica,* 143–44)[9]

(Two languages. The reality of uprooting (I use this term to indicate complete eradication) involves various problems or traumas, first of all that of a new language. As we progress in the acquisition of a foreign language, do we run the risk, for reasons of human vanity, of considering our mother tongue inferior? ...

One doesn't fall into this danger if the phenomenon of bilingualism is considered not as an achievement but as a forced denial of one's origins and of oneself. Bilingualism, that is, becomes synonymous with a disintegrated family unit, where a mother is no longer able to understand her own child. From the day the child says "Mother" for "mamma" and "sky" for "cielo," there is already a spiritual separation between mother and child that the linguistics scholar cannot categorize. If words are articulated sounds that symbolize and communicate an idea, the term "mamma," unlike "mother," the newly acquired term, symbolizes and communicates a whole world of feelings that no foreign expression can understand and respect. To abolish it is to reject the existence

---

[9] See his "Song of the Bicentennial," in *Gente Mia and Other Poems.*

of a childhood intimately linked to all the episodes, small and large, and to all the emotions, important and unimportant, connected to and inspired by that single word. Not assimilation or Americanization, therefore, but ambivalence, an ambivalence of thought and feeling, of doubt and certainty, of dream and reality.)

The consequence of this transformation is that the immigrant, in expressing him/herself in the acquired language, translates not only the words but also his/her soul and in that process of translation slowly and tirelessly begins to change. Now he/she is in possession of the language and culture of two countries: "America Italy; in what order, however! Shouldn't we say: Italy America?" (*La parola antica*, 143) Tusiani asks himself these questions because he believes that the immigrant cannot be completely assimilated into the acquired culture:

> Posta in termini diversi la domanda è: fino a qual punto l'emigrato può assimilare la nuova lingua e la nuova civiltà, e in che maniera dimenticare e rinnegare sé stesso in mezzo alle nuove e impellenti esigenze della sua vita? Anche se la risposta sia priva di validità scientifica, il poeta ci dice che non esiste, e non può esistere, un assorbimento totale, e che non potrà mai esserci un'accettazione totale, cioè *spirituale*, delle tradizioni della nuova terra. (*La parola antica* 143; my emphasis)

(Put in different terms, the question is: to what extent can the emigrant assimilate into the new language and new civilization, and in what way can he forget and deny himself in the midst of the new and pressing demands of his life? Even if the answer has no scientific validity, the poet tells us that there is not, and cannot be, total absorption, and that there can never be total, i.e., spiritual, acceptance of the traditions of the new land.)

Tusiani's continued feeling of "uprootedness" consists above all in the fact that he never integrated spiritually into American culture. This feeling is expressed very well in the episode that concludes *La parola antica*, the last volume of the trilogy. It figures as a significant episode to illustrate the dilemma of a writer between two worlds and who, all things considered, never renounces his Italian identity. Tusiani tells us that, returning from Italy, he dreams of finding himself with his mother in a long corridor illuminated by a blinding white light with many doors on both sides. At each end of the corridor there are two more doors, one labeled with the word "Exit" and the other "Entrance." Tusiani and his mother begin to walk toward the door marked "Exit." When they reach the end, they realize that the door now says "Entrance," and turning around they see that on the opposite door instead of "Entrance" it says "Exit."

> Arrivai sotto quella scrittura e lessi "Entrata." Mi voltai e vidi, lì dov'era mia madre, la parola "Uscita". ... Rifeci il cammino, ma quando raggiunsi mia madre, in alto, al posto di "Uscita" lessi nuovamente "Entrata"

... E per quaranta volte, affannato, ansioso, con la speranza e la disperazione che mi spingevano e guidavano, corsi da un'estremità all'altra di quell' enorme corridoio. (308)

(I reached the bottom of the writing and read "Entrance." I turned around and saw, where my mother had been, the word "Exit." [...] I retraced my steps, but when I reached my mother, at the top, instead of "Exit" I again read "Entrance." [...] And then forty times, breathless, anxious, with hope and despair pushing and guiding me, I ran from one end of that huge corridor to the other.)

Gripped with terror, Tusiani looks at the doors on either side of the hallway and notices that on each door is written the name of a person who has had a strong influence on his life. He knocks on each door, but no one answers. Finally, in the light, he sees the shadow of his father, who had died some years earlier:

"Papà! Papà!"gli dissi, andandogli incontro, "Ci siamo perduti io e mamma; non possiamo trovare l'uscita."
"Sei proprio un bambino," mi rispose mio padre, sorridendo. "So io dov'è l'uscita: venite con me." Cominciavamo a seguirlo. (309)

("Papa! Papa!" I said, walking up to him, "Mama and I are lost; we can't find our way out."
"You are such a child," my father replied, smiling. "I know where the exit is: Come with me." We began to follow him.)

At that point Tusiani is awakened by the flight attendant announcing his arrival in New York City. It seems that no one can help Tusiani locate the "Exit"; this is an existential problem to which only he can find the answer. The book, and the autobiography, ends with this short paragraph:

> Andando verso il Bronx, nella limousine della Poten [la ditta petroliera di suo fratello], notai un altro particolare: i tergicristalli, strusciando da destra a sinistra, da sinistra a destra, sembravano dire Entrata-Uscita, Uscita-Entrata, ma non sapevo più che cosa significassero quelle due parole, né a chi fossero rivolte. (310)

> (Heading toward the Bronx, in the limo of Poten [his brother's oil company], I noticed another detail: the windshield wipers, swiping from right to left, left to right, seemed to say Entrance-Exit, Exit-Entry, but I no longer knew what those two words meant or to whom they were addressed.)

A careful reading of this last paragraph suggests that Tusiani has finally arrived at a resolution of his immigrant problem. The resolution is the realization that he is suspended between two worlds, reacquainted with his biculturalism and accepting himself as a man of two languages and two sociocultural souls.

CONCLUSION (in a manner of speaking): A critical and comprehensive history of Italian American literature and culture has yet to be written, but the operation is underway. In this essay, following Paolo Valesio's suggestions, I have attempted to trace through texts that I consider exemplary and without, however, mentioning writers such as John Fante, Pietro Di Donato, Mario Puzo, and Giose Rimanelli (about whom much has been written), various stages in the development of Italian American fiction related to the phenomenon of the great emigration 1880–1924 and to make my own small contribution to this ongoing operation. The four texts chosen cover a period of sixty-five years. In their books, the authors examine the main themes surrounding emigration: the spiritually and psychologically violent act of separation from family and homeland (i.e., the first experience of the new emigrant), the dreams of the emigrant, the prejudices he encounters, the process of assimilation, the question (or rather the problem) of language, alienation and the eventual search for Italian roots and identity, and the realization that the new world is not always the land of hospitality that s/he believed it was to be.

REFERENCES

Barolini, Helen. 1979. *Umbertina*. New York: Seaview Press. Republished in 1999 by Feminist Press with an afterword by Edvige Giunta.

Barolini, Helen. 1985. The Dream Book: An Anthology of Writing by Italian American Women. Schocken.

Basile-Green, Rose. 1974. *The Italian-American Novel: A Document of the Interaction of Two Cultures.* Fairleigh Dickinson University Press, 1974.

Boelhower, William. 1981. "The Immigrant Novel as Genre," in *Melus.* 8.1: 3–14.

Boelhower, William. 1982. *Immigrant Autobiography in the United States.* Venice: Essedue.

Boelhower, William. 1984. *Through a Glass Darkly: Ethnic Semiosis.* New York: Oxford University Press.

Campisi, Paul. 1948. "Ethnic Family Patterns: The Italian Family in the United States." *American Journal of Sociology* 53.6: 443–449.

D'Agostino, Guido. *Olives on the Apple Tree.* New York: Amo Press Reprint, 1975.

D'Angelo, Pascal. *Son of Italy.* New York: Macmillan, 1924. Published subsequently by Guernica Editions in 2003.

di Donato, Pietro. 1939. *Christ in Concrete.*

Gardaphé, Fred L. 1992. "My House Is Not Your House: Jerre Mangione and Italian-American Autobiography," *Multicultural Autobiography American Lives*, James Robert Payne, ed. University of Tennessee Press. 139–177.

Gardaphé, Fred L. 1996. *Italian Signs American Streets: The Evolution of Italian American Narrative.* Duke University Press.

Giunta, Edvige. 1995. "Blending 'Literary' Discourses: Helen Barolini's Italian/American Narratives," *Romance Languages Annual* 6.

Giunta, Edvige. 1999. "Afterword, An Immigrant Tapestry." In Helen Barolini's *Umbertina*. New York: Feminist Press.

Kotsaftis, Maria. 2000. "A Female Odyssey in Quest of the Self," *Adjusting Sites: New Essays in Italian American Studies*, William Boelhower, ed. Stony Brook, NY: FILibrary.

Lopreato, Joseph. 1970. *Italian Americans*. New York: Random House.
Marchand, Jean-Jacques. 1992. *La letteratura dell'emigrazione. Scrittori di lingua italiana nel mondo*. Edizioni della Fondazione Giovanni Agnelli.
Puzo, Mario. 1965. *The Fortunate Pilgrim*. New York: Atheneum, 1965.
Puzo, Mario. 1969. *The Godfather*. New York: G. P. Putnam, 1969.
Tamburri, Anthony Julian. 1991a. "*Umbertina*: The Italian-American Woman's Experience." In *From the Margin: Writings in Italian Americana*, eds. Anthony Julian Tamburri, Paolo A. Giordano, and Fred L. Gardaphé. West Lafayette, IN: Purdue University Press. 357–375.
Tamburri, Anthony Julian. 1991b. *To Hyphenate or Not to Hyphenate: The Italian-American Writer An Other American*. Montreal: Guernica, 1991.
Tamburri, Anthony Julian. 1998. *A Semiotic of Ethnicity: In (Re)cognition of the Italian/American Writer*. Albany, NY: SUNY Press.
Tamburri, Anthony Julian, Paolo A. Giordano, and Fred L. Gardaphé, eds. 2000, 2nd edition (1991). *From the Margin: Writings in Italian Americana*. Purdue University Press.
Tusiani, Joseph. 1978. "Song of the Bicentennial," in *Gente Mia and Other Poems*. Stone Park, IL: Italian Cultural Center. Now as *Ethnicity. Selected Poems*, edited with two essays by Paolo Giordano. Lafayette: Bordighera Press, 2000.
Tusiani, Joseph. 1988. *La parola difficile: Autobiography of an Italian-American*. Fasano: Schena.
Tusiani, Joseph. 1991. *La parola nuova: Autobiography of an Italian-American*. Fasano: Schena.
Tusiani, Joseph. 1992. *La parola antica: Autobiography of an Italian-American*. Fasano: Schena.

Valesio, Paolo. 1989. "Writer Between Two Worlds: Italian Writing in the United States Today." *Differentia* 3-4: 259–276.

Viscusi, Robert. 1981. "*De vulgari eloquentia*: An Approach to the Language of Italian American Fiction." *Yale Italian Studies* 1.3: 21–38.

Part II

Italiana

Gabriello Chiabrera
An Overview

Benedetto Croce opened a new chapter in Italian Baroque criticism in 1929 by pointing to the common aspects of the poetics of Giambattista Marino and Gabriello Chiabrera, who are generally considered the most important poets of the period. Although quite different in their approaches, Croce argued that both writers were in search of a style that would produce in readers a reaction of startled amazement. Like many Baroque writers, they took their inspiration from an understanding of reality that was profoundly different from that of the sixteenth century. This new worldview was created by the Council of Trent, the emergence of new science, and the discovery of the New World.

Chiabrera was equally at home in composing heroic poems, poems about everyday life, love poems, occasional poems, popular poems, and poems on sub. lime topics. This wide range of interests goes far to explain his long-lasting fame, which did not wane until the twentieth century. He was a friend of such luminaries as Ansaldo Cebà and Pier Giuseppe Giustiniani, both of whom were members of the Genoese Accademia degli Addormentati (Academy of the Sleepy Heads); a close friend and collaborator of the Florentine writers Roberto Titi and Gian Battista Strozzi and the renowned librettist Ottavio Rinuccini; and acquainted with the poets Fulvio Testi, Carlo de'Dottori, and Francesco Redi and the satirist Benedetto Menzini. He is considered alongside with Alessandro Guidi and Francesco De Lemene, a precursor of the eighteenth-century Arcadian literary movement.

Chiabrera was born in Savona on 18 June 1552. His father, Gabriello, died before he was born, and his mother, Geronima Murassana, remarried soon afterward. Chiabrera's paternal uncle Giovanni and his wife, Margherita, assumed responsibility for Chiabrera's upbringing and brought him to live with them in Rome when he was nine. He was educated by private tutors and then at the Jesuit Collegio Romano. In Rome he met many prominent cultural figures but was especially influenced by Paolo Manunzio, a renowned philologist and classical scholar who lived next door to his uncle: Marc Antoine Muret. a friend of the French poet Pierre de Ronsard and a translator of Ronsard's works; and, above all, the critic, dramatist, and philosopher Sperone Speroni. Chiabrera met Torquato Tasso, the author of the epic poem *Gerusalemme* liberata (1581, Jerusalem Delivered; translated as *Godfrey of Bulloigne, or The Recouerie of Hierusalem*, 1594) at Speroni's home in December 1575.

After his uncle's death in 1572, Chiabrera entered the service of Cardinal Luigi Cornaro, but he had to leave Rome and return to Savona in 1579 because of a violent controversy with a Roman nobleman. His combative personality caused him further problems in Savona. Between 1579 and 1581 and again in 1583 he was forced to leave that city to avoid incarceration and bodily harm. He returned to Savona in 1585 and lived there in relative tranquility for the rest of his life.

Chiabrera embarked on his writing career with the heroic poem *Delle guerre dei Goti* (The War of the Goths), which was published in Venice in 1582 and dedicated to Carlo Emanuele I, Duke of Savoy. In fifteen eight-line cantos it deals with the last two months of the war in which the Greeks and Italians defeated the Ostrogoths in 553 and sings the praises of Vitiello, the Roman knight entrusted by heaven with the victory. After their king, Teia, is killed, the Goths surrender their arms and are allowed to live in peace under their own laws. The subtext of the poem is the contemporary conflict between the Roman Catholic Church and the northern Reformers.

During his long life Chiabrera produced a vast quantity of lyrical, epic, tragic, pastoral, and satirical verse, but his reputation as one of the two best poets of the Italian literary Baroque is mainly based on his lyrical compositions: three volumes of *Canzoni* (1586-1588. Canzones). *Canzonette* (1591. Canzonets). *Le maniere dei versi toscani* (1599, The Style of Tuscan Verses), *Scherzi e canzonette morali* (1599, Scherzi and Moral Canzonets), and "Le vendemmie di Parnaso" (1605, Harvests in Parnassus). Like that of Marino, Chiabrera's poetry is innovative and creates a sense of meraviglia (wonder in the reader. but unlike Marino and the Marinists, who create this sense through an abundance of extravagant metaphors and witty conceits, Chiabrera shifts the emphasis from imagery to form by using classical Greek and Latin metric schemes. Although he read widely and was well versed in the classical canon, his major influences were Pindar, Anacreon, Horace, and Catullus. His understanding of classical literature was filtered through his reading of Ronsard, the preeminent poet of the avant-garde Pléiade movement. The Pléiade aimed to create a new poetry that would make a decisive break from the moribund medieval tradition, enrich French by composing verse in that language instead of in Latin, and equal or surpass works of the classical period and the Italian Renaissance. The more than 180 canzones in Chiabrera's 1586-1588 and 1599 volumes can be divided into four thematic groups: 95 praise the exploits of heroes; 16 are mournful or funereal and are dedicated to fallen heroes; 44 impart a moral lesson and deprecate vice and error; and 20 are *canzoni sacre* (sacred compositions) honoring Christian saints and martyrs.

Chiabrera's heroic verses consecrate the election of popes, sing the praises of winners of athletic contests, and celebrate the victories of Christian knights over "infidels." He had great confidence in his poetic talent and referred to himself as the Italian Pindar; his canzones use classical topoi and have constant recourse to myth. Among the laudatory canzones are odes in celebration of Emanuele Filiberto, Duke of Savoy, reformer of the Savoyard state and winner of the Battle of San Quentin in Picardy in 1556; Christopher Columbus; and Enrico Dandolo, doge of Venice from 1192 to 1205, who led the Fourth Crusade and the conquest of Constantinople and was regarded by many as the true founder of the Venetian empire.

Chiabrera's myths are not simply ornaments to display the poet's erudition but are necessary structural components of the odes and a means of amplifying the praise of the heroes. Well-known tales from the Homeric repertory and of the labors of Hercules appear alongside less familiar stories of metamorphoses and magic. Chiabrera's champions are immersed in the classical world of heroes and heroines, gods and demigods, Achilles and Jason, and the Odyssey and the Iliad: his subjects and the heroes of classical antiquity become one and the same; the exploits and virtues of his champions become the exploits and virtues of their classical counterparts. Where the subject matter does not allow for the use of classical pagan mythology, as in the compositions in praise of popes, Chiabrera substitutes grandiose and marvelous episodes from the Bible.

Poetry and the poet are also celebrated in Chiabrera's canzones. For example, the canzone on Emanuele Filiberto opens with a brief reference to locality and landscape, after which Chiabrera describes his duty as a poet, expresses confidence in his skill, and extols his role as a writer of encomiastic poetry that is destined to astonish the reader in the same way as the exploits it depicts: "io meco ho strali avuti / che sanno altrui ferir di maraviglia" (I have with me sharp darts / that can wound others with the wondrous).

The canzones also include war songs that celebrate the naval victories of the Tuscan galleys over the "infidels." Representative is the canzone dedicated to the battle of Bona (today Annaba) on the coast of Algeria (called Libya in the text), in which Florentine ships had taken part:

> Con qual dunque corona
> bella Flora, nel sen delle tue mura
> farassi onore eterno al di presente,
> in cui l'orribil Bona
> dentro nembo di pianto il ciglio oscura
> per gli assalti di tua nobil gente?
> Certo di dedalei marmi
> Déi scolpir di sì bell'armi.

> (Then, with what crown
> beautiful Flora, within the womb of your walls
> will you today bestow eternal honor,
> now that terrible Bona
> darkens the sky with clouds of its tears
> for the fierce attacks of your noble people?

Certainly in Daedalean marble
You must sculpt so great a fleet.)

Chiabrera goes on to praise the commander of the fleet, Grand Duke Cosimo I de' Medici:

E se feroce in guerra
Cosmo ara il mare, ed orgogliosi liti
fa tremare il suo nome in strani modi.

(If fiercely as in war
Cosimo sails the sea, proud shores
will tremble at the sound of his name.)

He compares Cosimo to Jason, who sailed with the Argonauts in search of the Golden Fleece to reclaim the throne of Iolkos from the usurper Pelia.

In another poem Chiabrera praises Columbus for persisting against all odds, not being deterred by his detractors, and ardently believing in the truth of his ideas:

L'ocean corse, e i turbini sostenne
vinse le crude immagini di morte;
poscia dell'ampio mar spenta la guerra,
scorse dianzi favolosa terra.

Allor del cavo Pin scende veloce,
e di gran orma il nuovo mondo imprime;
né men ratto per l'aria erge sublime,
segno del Ciel, l'insuperabil Croce.

(He sailed the oceans and withstood storms
He overcame crude images of death;
After he won the war against an expansive sea,
he saw the fabled land in front of him.

From his ship he quickly descends
and with historical footprints he marked the New World;
and as quickly he erects a sublime sign
of heaven, the unexcelled Cross.)

Columbus's well-earned triumph is that of a heroic devout Christian who conquers the ocean and discovers a new world not for himself but for his country and all of humanity.

In the canzones Chiabrera employs a learned vocabulary, Hellenisms, rhetorical figures, anaphoras, parallel-isms, antitheses, and iterations to create a vigorous but solemn language capable of transmitting a wide variety of feelings from the most exalted to the desperate cries of the afflicted and downtrodden. The latter can be found in his intense and dramatic apostrophe to a personified Italy:

Ma tu qual trarrai pianto
e quali Italia gemiti infiniti
misera madre degli eroi traditi?

(But you, what tears, what infinite wails
will you draw, oh Italy,
wretched mother of betrayed heroes?)

Three of Chiabrera's *canzoni sacre* are dedicated to the martyred Sicilian St. Lucy, to whom he also alludes in other writings.

In 1590 Chiabrera composed the tragedy *Ippodamia*, which was posthumously published in 1794. It is based on the episode in Homer's *Iliad* in which Priam's daughter, Polyxena, lures Achilles into an ambush by Paris.

During the last two decades of the century Chiabrera largely devoted himself to the composition of canzonets, his first collection of which was published in 1591. In his autobiography, "Vita scritta da lui medesimo" (1718, Life Written by Himself), and in the dialogue "Il Geri: Della tessitura delle canzoni" (1952, Geri: On the Composition of Canzones) he states that his main sources of inspiration for the canzonets were Anacreon and Ronsard. His principal motivation for turning to the genre was his desire to have his poetry set to music; short verses are easier to sing:

Dolcissimo ben mio
io ben come desio
ognor posso adorarti
ma non posso lodarti
ognor come desio,
dolcissimo ben mio.

(Sweet love of mine
I fully desire thee
every hour I adore thee
but I cannot praise thee
every hour as I wish,
Sweet love of mine.)

He also wanted to attract the new reading public of young men and women who had no taste for the serious and solemn songs of Dante and Petrarch. In poems such as the celebrated "Belle rose porporine" (Beautiful Vermillion Roses) he creates a blend of images and sounds that intoxicate the senses:

Se bel rio se bell'auretta
tra lerbetta
sul mattin mormorando erra:
se di fiori un praticello
si fa bello
noi diciam: ride la terra.

(If a clear stream, if a soft breeze
through the grass
in the morning wanders murmuring;
if a meadow with flowers
makes itself beautiful
we say: the earth laughs.)

In the canzonet "Sono da schivarsi gli affanni" (Worries Are to Be Avoided) Chiabrera exhorts the painter Il Bronzino (Angelo Allori) to enjoy and immerse himself in the present; worrying about what he cannot control will not solve the problems that beset the world or change the course of history. "O da ricrearsi nelle stagioni noiose" (One Must Amuse Oneself during the Midday Hours) creates a vivid scene of recreational delights such as floating lazily on a boat and fishing for octopus with a trident to while away the hot, humid afternoon hours. The pain that love brings is described in "Dissuade amore" (Deters from Loving), as well as in "Non vuole più amare la sua donna" (He No Longer Wants to Love His Lady):

> In van lusinghimi
> in van minaccimi,
> figlio di venere:
> quel giogo impostomi
> dolce o spiacevole
> i più nol vo.

> (In vain you deceive me
> in vain you threaten me,
> son of Venus:
> the game you impose on me
> sweet or unpleasant
> I do not seek anymore.)

In *Scherzi e canzonette morali*, dedicated to the Florentine playwright Iacopo Cicognini, Chiabrera expresses the desire to spend the rest of his days in healthy idleness, far from the pomp and splendor of the Roman curia. He praises the quiet pastoral life and condemns courtly rituals:

> Io solitario, e fin dagli anni acerbi
> uso alle selve, odio palagi alteri,
> né soffro onda di duci in su destrieri,
> e grandi in toga pareggiar superbi.
>
> (In solitude, from my earliest years
> I loved the countryside, and hated haughty palaces,
> Nor can I suffer waves of dukes on their steeds,
> nor great men in togas in arrogant competition.)

Chiabrera is content in his solitude and feels close to nature; but his longing for recognition as a great poet who celebrates great men is still alive.

The canzonets received critical praise from the Arcadian poets and from critics and scholars of the eighteenth and nineteenth centuries. Francesco De Sanctis, who was generally harsh in his judgment of Chiabrera's works, regarded the canzonets as the only poems by Chiabrera that were worth reading.

In 1600, Chiabrera was invited to Florence to participate in the wedding festivities of Maria de' Medici and King Henry IV of France. The celebration was crowned with a presentation of his *Il rapimento di Cefalo* (The Abduction of Cephalus), set to music by Giulio Caccini. By the beginning of the seventeenth century Chiabrera's literary accomplishments began to be recognized and rewarded. He received honors from the dukes of Savoy, Mantua, and Florence; Pope Urban VIII; the Republic of Genoa; and Grand Duke Ferdinando I de' Medici of Tuscany, who in 1600 conferred on him the title Gentiluomo del Granduca (Gentleman of the Grand Duke) and a monthly stipend that required little work on Chiabrera's part. From 1600 until his death, he also held various minor civil appointments in Florence.

Chiabrera's pastoral drama *Gelopea* (1604) is modeled on Battista Guarini's *Il Pastor fido* (1590; translated as *Il pastor fido*; or *The Faithful Shepherd*, 1602). The rivalry between Filebo, a poor shepherd boy, and Berillo, a farm laborer, for the hand of Gelopea, the daughter of a rich and powerful shepherd, is an allusion to the conflict between the wealthy merchants and the impoverished Genoese nobility. With the marriage of Filebo and Gelopea, Chiabrera proposes a solution based on tolerance, love, and reconciliation.

Chiabrera's *Rime* (1605, Rhymes) includes "Vendemmie in Parnaso," fifty-three bacchic odes of 7 to 132 verses in which the speaker invites his friends to drink in the refined atmosphere of an aristocratic country villa: "Beviam, a diansi al vento / i torbidi pensieri.... Beviam, che non è ria / ogni gentil follia" (Let's drink, and abandon to the wind / our troubled thoughts. Let's drink, gentle folly / is not a wicked thing). Modeled on classical Greek poetry, Chiabrera's bacchic poems replace the themes of youthful and playful love in the canzonets with a celebration of the enjoyment of fine wines that is more consonant with the tranquility of middle age. Referring to the mourning of Venus for the death of Adonis, a popular myth of tragic love, Chiabrera writes, "A Si detto fatto / alla mia man ricorda / che per canto d'amor non tocchi corda" (This well-known event / reminds my hand / not to touch the strings of love's song). Wine is the remedy for the pain of unhappy love: "Sciocchezze! Con buon vin cangia la donna / Bevi gagliardo fin che il ciglio assonna" (Fool-ishness! Good wine changes the woman / Drink, brave man, until sleep's onset). In poem 48, "Aure serene e chiare" (Calm and Clear Breezes), set in the countryside, the speaker offers a woman a precious cup adorned with images:

> Sulla sponda romita
> lungo il bel rio di questa riva erbosa,
> o Filli, a bere invita
> ostro vivo di fragola odorosa.
>
> Fra mie tazze pij care
> reca la più diletta
> quella dove saetta
> Amor sopra un delfin gli dei del mare.

(On the solitary mound
along the grassy shore of this beautiful river,
oh Filli, the clear purple of strawberry wine
invites us to drink.

Among my most precious goblets
I brought the most beloved
the one where Love on a dolphin
darts across the sea.)

The poems include references to regional wines, caves that serve as natural wine cellars, guests, hunts, greyhounds, and the hills surrounding Chiabrera's native Savona.

Chiabrera believed that the theater should be made accessible to as wide an audience as possible by drawing on popular literary works. Accordingly, his second tragedy, Erminia, also included in Rime, is adapted from Tasso's *Gerusalemme liberata* and completes the story of the Saracen princess Erminia, who commits suicide after the Christian knight Tancredi rejects her love.

Meganira (1608), the least known and least successful of Chiabrera's three pastoral dramas, draws from Tasso's *Aminta* (1573: translated, 1591) the motif of the false death of the protagonist. His third pastoral play, Alcippo (1614), uses the stock situation of the shepherd dressed in women's clothes. In the guise of Megilla, Alcippo enters the community of nymphs to try to persuade the huntress Clori to abandon her way of life and consider marriage. Alcippo's true identity is discovered; the law requires the intruder to be put to death; Clori's compromised honor will have to be vindicated; and her right to live the life she has chosen must be restored. A tragic resolution is avoided by the recognition of Alcippo as the long-believed-dead son of the elder Tirsi. Clori, who was born to humble parents, consents to the marriage to Alcippo proposed by Tirsi and the high priest Montano out of gratitude to those who brought her up and protected her. But the happy ending is marred by Clor's lack of enthusiasm: resigned to her fate, she accepts the restrictions imposed by a patriarchal society that condemns women to live a life chosen for them: "che più dirvi degg'io? / Sia nelle vostre mani, e voi reggete il freno / di ciascun mio desio" (What more can I say to you? / I am in your hands / and you hold the reins / to all my desires). The plots of Gelopea, Meganira, and Alcippo reflect the conservative rural setting where the Genoese aristocracy spent its leisure time.

Chiabrera's final tragedy, *Angelica in Ebuda* (1615), is adapted from Ludovico Ariosto's chivalric poem *Orlando furioso* (1516, Orlando Enraged; translated as Orlando Furioso in English Heroical Verse, 1591). It dramatizes the capture of the pagan princess Angelica by the monstrous Orc and her rescue by the African knight Ruggiero and a flying horse. Chiabrera's tragedies were not as well received as his pastoral dramas;

his attempt to write dramas based on popular literature to attract a wider public was premature. Reform of the Italian tragic theater in this direction was accomplished by the Arcadian Metastasio (Pietro Trapassi) with his sentimental melodramas of the early eighteenth century.

Chiabrera had conceived the idea of an epic poem in honor of the House of Savoy in 1582 and had begun writing it in 1590. He submitted the manuscript for the first version to his patron, Carlo Emanuele I, in 1607. Three years later he presented the duke a revised version of the poem, expanded to twelve cantos. He gave the duke another revised and enlarged version in 1617. In 1629 he revised it a third time, enlarged it to 1,335 octaves in twenty-three cantos, and published it as the Amedeide. The hero of the *Amedeide* is Count Amedeo V, who, according to legend, defended the island of Rhodes from the Turks in the early fourteenth century. In the final battle, described in great detail in cantos 19 through 21, Amedeo kills the Turkish king Ottoman. In the final canto St. John, the Baptist predicts the future glories of Dukes Emanuele Filiberto and Carlo Emanuele I. Chiabrera's most ambitious and complex work, the *Amedeide* was reduced to ten cantos in a fourth revision, published in 1635.

Il Firenze (Florence) is Chiabrera's other major contribution to the epic genre; it was published in octaves in ten cantos in 1615 and dedicated to Cosimo II de'

Medici, Grand Duke of Tuscany. He expanded it to fifteen cantos and recast it in unrhymed eleven-syllable lines for the second edition, dedicated to Ferdinand II de' Medici, in 1628 and reduced it to ten cantos for the third edition in 1637. The poem celebrates the coming to power of the Medici dynasty in the mid ninth century. The pious Christian hero, Cosmo, liberates Florence from submission to the neighboring city of Fiesole, ruled by the godless and dissolute King Feralmo.

Two other epic poems — *Foresto*, three cantos in octaves on Attila the Hun, and *Ruggiero*, ten cantos in unrhymed verse on the character from *Orlando furioso* — were published posthumously in 1653. Chiabrera also composed at least thirty-two *poemetti* (much shorter heroic poems with less intricate plots) on both sacred and profane topics. He participated in one of the most important literary debates of his time, the reform of the epic genre, in his dialogue "Vecchietti: Intorno al verso eroico volgare" (1952, Vecchietti: On the Vernacular Heroic Verse) and in many letters. He advocated the adoption of the classical precept of unity of action and the use of hendecasyllabic blank verse.

&

In the last twenty years of his life Chiabrera seldom left Savona except for pleasure trips and occasional visits to the courts of princes who summoned him. In 1625 he wrote the short autobiography "Vita scritta da lui medesimo," which was published posthumously in

1718. Referring to himself in the third person, he offers an idealized account of his life.

Between 1624 and 1632 Chiabrera composed thirty satirical poems that were collected in 1718 as "Sermoni" (Sermons). While most of his predecessors identified satire with the self-righteous invective of the Roman writer Juvenal, Chiabrera's satires are in the familiar and whimsical vein of Horace and Ariosto; some take the form of letters addressed to real-life friends. Expressing a mature wisdom that is only rarely tainted by acrimony, Chiabrera condemns the pursuit of fame and wealth, praises the simple country life, laments the corruption of the judicial system, and deplores the ravages of modern warfare. The "Sermoni" are composed in unrhymed eleven-syllable lines rather than terza rima, the traditional meter of Italian satirical poetry. Chiabrera's satires were much admired by later Italian practitioners of the genre such as Giuseppe Parini and Giacomo Leopardi. Chiabrera died on 14 October 1638.

In his autobiography Gabriello Chiabrera wrote that he tried to follow Columbus in discovering a "new world" of poetry in reaction to the tired and lackluster Petrarchism of his time and what he considered its degenerate poetic style, and his lyrics paved the way for the Arcadian reform of Italian poetry and drama. While he declared himself opposed to the use of traditional fixed-rhyme structures and wrote some of his longer poems in blank verse, he introduced metrical and strophic innovations adopted from classical literatures that had a long-lasting influence on Italian poetry. The grave and solemn style of his heroic and moral poems and the light, musical style of the canzonet brought him accolades during his lifetime and assured him a place in the annals of seventeenth-century Italian literature alongside Marino.

Bibliography

Books:

Delle guerre dei Goti. Venice: Gioacchino Brugnolo, 1582.
Delle Canzoni, 3 volumes. Genoa: Girolamo Bartoli, 1586-1588.
Canzonette. Genoa: Girolamo Bartoli, 1591.
Le maniere dei versi toscani. Genoa: Giuseppe Pavoni, 1599.
Scherzi e canzonette morali. Genoa: Giuseppe Pavoni, 1599.
Rime. Genoa: Giuseppe Pavoni, 1599.
Il rapimento di Cefalo: Rappresentato nelle nozze della cristianissima Maria Medici Regina di Francia è di Navarra, music by Giulio Caccini. Florence: Giorgio Marescotti, 1600.
Narrazione della morte di S. Gio. Batista. Florence: Giunti, 1602.
Herodiate. Florence: Giunti, 1602.
Alcuni scherzi. Mondov: De Rossi, 1603.
Rime sacre. Genoa: Francesco Bolzeta, 1604.
Gelopea. Mondovi: De Rossi, 1604.
Rime. Venice: Sebastiano Combi, 1605. includes "Le vendemmie di Parnaso" and Erminia.
Poesie, 3 volumes. Genoa: Giuseppe Pavoni, 1605-1606.
Egloghe. Florence: Giorgio Antonio Caneo, 1608.
Meganira. Florence: Giorgio Antonio Caneo, 1608.
Alcippo: Favola boschereccia. Genoa: Giuseppe Pavoni, 1614.

Alcune canzoni composte per la corte di Toscana. Florence: Giorgio Antonio Canco, 1615.
Favolette da rappresentarsi cantando. Florence: Pignoni, 1615.
Il pianto di Orfeo. Florence: Pignoni, 1615.
Angelica in Ebuda. Florence: Pignoni, 1615.
Il Firenze. Florence: Pignoni, 1615; enlarged edition, Florence: Ciotti, 1628; revised, 1637.
Vegghia delle Grazie. Florence: Caneo, 1616.
Poesie, 3 volumes. Florence: Pignoni, 1618.
Il presagio dei giorni. Florence: Pignoni, 1618.
Versi, Meteore. Florence: Cecconcelli, 1618.
Il vivaio dei Boboli. Genoa: Giuseppe Pavoni, 1620.
Per San Carlo Borromeo. Genoa: Giuseppe Pavoni, 1620.
Amedeide. Genoa: Giuseppe Pavoni, 1620: revised edition, Naples, 1635.
Galatea o le grotte di Fassolo. Genoa: Giuseppe Pavoni, Il Forzano. Alessandria: G. Soto, 1626.
Poesie, 4 volumes. Florence: Ciotti, 1628.
Foresto. Genoa: Guasco, 1653.
Ruggiero. Genoa: Guasco, 1653.
Discorsi fatti da Gabriello Chiabrera nell'Academia degli Addormentuti in Genova, edited by Alessandro Dego. Genoa: Franchello, 1670.
Rime, edited by G. Paolucci. Rome: Salvioni, 1718. includes "Vita scritta da lui medesimo" and "Sermomi"
Alcune boesie di Gabriele Chiabrera non mai prima d'ora pubblicate. edited by Olimpio Fenicio. Genoa: Caffarelli, 1784.
Canzonette, rime varie, dialoghi di Gabriello Chiabrera, edited by Luigi Negri. Turin: Einaudi, 1952.

EDITIONS AND COLLECTIONS
Sermoni... aggiunte le asservazioni di Clementino Vannetti. Genoa, 1830.

Il rapimento di Cefalo, in *Gli Albori del melodramma,* volume 3 by A. Solerti. Milan, Palermo & Naples: Sandron, 1904.

I lirici del Seicento e dell'Arcadia, edited by Carlo Calcaterra. Milan: Rizzoli, 1936.

Poesia del Seicento, volume 1, edited by Carlo Muscetta and Pier Paolo Ferrante. Turin: Einaudi, 1964. 690-734;

Opere di Gabriello Chiabrera e lirici del classicismo barocco, edited by Marcello Turchi. Turin: Unione Tipografico-Editrice Torinese, 1984. 523-616;

Gelopea: Favola boschereccia, edited by Franco Vazzoler. Genoa: Marietti, 1988.

Edition in English

From Marino to Marinetti: An Anthology of Forty Italian Poets, translated by Joseph Tusiani. New York: Baroque Press, 1974. 15-23.

PLAY PRODUCTION

Il rapimento di Cefalo, music by Giulio Caccini, Florence, 1600.

LETTERS

Lettere di Gabriello Chiabrera, edited by Giacomo Filippo Porrata. Bologna: Printed by Lelio dalla Volpe for the Istituto delle Scienze, 1672.

Ottavio Varaldo, "Rime e lettere inedite di Gabriello Chiabrera," *Atti e memorie della società storica savonese,* 1. (1888): 281-349; 2 (1889-1890): 395-424.

Lettere (1585-1638), edited by Simona Morando. Florence: Olschki, 2003.

BIBLIOGRAPHIES

Ottavio Varaldo, "Bibliografia delle opere a stampa di Gabriello Chiabrera," Giorale ligustico di archeologia, storia e letteratura, 13 (1886): 280-423.

Varaldo, "Bibliografia chiabreresca: Supplemento," Giorale ligustico di archeologia, storia e letteratura, 14 (1887): 406-425.

Severino Ferrari, Gabriello Chiabrera e le raccolte di rime da lui medesino ordinate: Studio bibliografico. Faenza: Conti, 1888.

Varaldo, "Bibliografia delle opere a stampa di Gabriello Chiabrera," Atti e memorie della società storica savonese, 2 (1889-1890): 425-457.

Gustavo Costa, "Gli autografi del Chiabrera presso la Biblioteca Vaticana (appunti critico-bibliografici con alcuni inediti," *Studi Secenteschi*, 8 (1967): 43-71.

Franco Vazzoler, "Lettere inedite di Gabriello Chiabrera," *La rassegna della letteratura italiana*, 73 (1969): 27-36.

BIOGRAPHY

Nicola Merola, "Gabriello Chiabrera," in *Dizionario biografico degli italiani*, volume 24, edited by Alberto M. Ghisalberti. Rome: Istituto dell'Enciclopedia Italiana, 1980: 465-475.

REFERENCES

Antonio Belloni, *Gli epigoni della* Gerusalemme liberate. Padua: Angelo Draghi, 1893): 32-46, 149-173.

Antonio Belloni, *Il Seicento*, second edition. Milan: Vallardi, 1955. 200-202, 394-395.

Giorgio Bertone, *Per una ricerca metricologica su Chiabrera*. Genoa: Marietti, 1991.

Giorgio Bertone, *Per una ricerca su Chiabrera*. Genoa: Marietti, 1988.

Fulvio Bianchi, "Gabriello Chiabrera," in *La letteratura ligure: La repubblica aristocratica (1528-1797)*, by Bianchi, Franco Arato, Franco Vazzoler, and others. Genoa: Costa & Nolan, 1988. 149-215.

Fulvio Bianchi, "Per una definizione critica del Chiabrera: Riflessioni su una questione ancora aperta," in *Studi di filologia e letteratura offerti a Franco Croce*. Florence: Bulzoni, 1997. 213-229.

Fulvio Bianchi and Paolo Rossi, eds., *La scelta della misura: Gabriello Chiabrera. L'altro fuoco del barocco italiano. Atti del Convegno di studi su Gabriello Chiabrera nel 350° anniversario della morte*: Savona, 3-6 novembre 1988. Genoa: Costa & Nolan, 1993.

Vittorio Cian, *La satira dall'Ariosto al Chiabrera*, volume 2, second edition. Milan: Vallardi, 1945.

Marco Corradini, *Genova e il barocco: Studi su Angelo Grillo, Ansaldo Cebà, Anton Giulio Brignole Sale*. Milan: Vita e Pensiero, 1994. 21-22, 25, 27-28, 56-66, 125, 132-133, 146, 238-239.

Benedetto Croce, *Storia dell'età barocca*. Bari: Laterza,1929. 281-284, 426-427.

Francesco De Sanctis, *Storia della letteratura*, edited by Croce. Bari: Laterza, 1958): 199-202.

Giovanni Getto, "Gabriello Chiabrera poeta barocco," in his *Barocco in prosa e in poesia*. Milan: Rizzoli, 1969. 123-162.

Enzo Noé Girardi, *Esperienza e poesia di Gabriello Chiabrera*. Milan: Vita e Pensiero, 1950.

Girardi, "Gabriello Chiabrera," in *Letteratura italiana: I minori*, volume 2. Milan: Marzorati, 1961. 1427-1147.

Carmine Iannaco and Martino Capucci, *Il Seicento*. Padua: Piccin Nuova Libraria, 1986. 228-251, 566-567.

Giacomo Jori, "Poesia lirica 'marinista e anti marinista': Fra classicismo e barocco," in *Storia della letteratura italiana*, volume 5, edited by Enrico Malato. Rome: Salerno Editore, 1997.

Albert N. Mancini, "Writing the Self: Forms of Autobiography in the Late Italian Renaissance," *Canadian Journal of Italian Studies*, 14 (1991): 11-22.

Francesco Luigi Mannucci, *La lirica di Gabriello Chiabrera: Storia e caratteri*. Naples, Genoa & Città di Castello: Francesco Perella, 1925.

Gian Piero Maragoni, "Gabriel in villa. Coup d'essay sul Chiabrera bucolico," *Dismisura* 12 (1983): 63-66.

Quinto Marini, "Orazio e i Sermoni di Gabriello Chiabrera," in *Orazio e la letteratura italiana: Contributi alla storia della fortuna del poeta latino. Atti del convegno svoltosi a Licenza dal 19 al 23 aprile 1993 nell'ambito delle celebrazioni del bimillenario della morte di Quito Orazio Flacco*. Rome: Istituto poligrafico e Zecca dello Stato, Liberia dello Stato, 1994. 241-276.

Ferdinando Neri, *Chiabrera e la Pléiade francese*. Turin: Bocca, 1920.

Marzia Pieri, "Vanità e onesti diletti: Il teatro di Gabriello Chiabrera," *Rassegna della letteratura italiana* 95 (1991): 5-20.

Franco Vazzoler, "Letteratura e ideologia aristocratica a Genova nel primo seicento," in *La letteratura ligure: La repubblica aristocratica (1528-1797)*, by Bianchi, Franco Arato, Franco Vazzoler, and others. Genoa: Costa & Nolan, 1988. 230-244.

2012: Paul receives the "Parmurelu d'oru" lifetime achievement award from the Descu Rundu Cultural Association of Bordighera, Italy. This is an annual award to an individual, born, resident, or traceable by his/her activities to Bordighera, who has honored the city's name and brought prestige to it in a specific field.

Beppe Fenoglio's Theatrical and Cinematic Writings: An Overview

Beppe Fenoglio died in 1963; he left a vast amount of unpublished material. This material, in various stages of incompleteness, has been conserved at the Fondo Fenoglio in Alba, the author's birthplace. Among numerous short stories, unfinished novels, epigrams, fables, and a diary, there is also evidence that he was adapting some of his prose for both the theater and the screen.

At the time of his unexpected death only a small portion of his work had been published: a few short stories had appeared in various journals and magazines: *I ventitre giorni della città di Alba* (Einaudi, 1952), a collection of twelve short stories on the Resistance and life in the *Langhe* region of Piedmont; *La malora* (Einaudi, 1954), a "racconto lungo" on life and poverty in the *Langhe*; a translation of Samuel Coleridge's *The Rhyme of the Ancient Mariner* (in *Itinerari*, 1955); *Primavera di bellezza* (Garzanti, 1955), a novel about growing up during the fascist era. Finally, all Fenoglio's narrative work, published and unpublished, was compiled by a team of scholars under the direction of Maria Corti of the Università di Pavia. It is a three-volume, five-tome edition that was published by Einaudi in 1978.

The *Opere* is divided as follows: I, 1, *Ur Partigiano Johnny*, edited by John Meddemmen and translated by Bruce Merry; I, 2, *Il partigiano Johnny*, edited by Maria Antonietta Grignani; I, 3, *Primavera di Bellezza, Frammenti di un romanzo*, and *Una questione privata*, edited by Maria Antonietta Grignani; II, *Racconti delta guerra civile, La paga del sabato, I ventitre giorni della città di Alba, La malora*, and *Un giorno di fuoco*, edited by Piera Tomasoni; III, *Racconti sparsi e inediti*, [*Quaderno Bonalumi*], [*Diario*], *Testi teatrali, Progetto di sceneggiatura cinematografica*, edited by Piera Tomasoni, *Epigrammi*, edited by Carla Maria Sanfilippo.[1]

Fenoglio's opus revolves around two major themes: 1) the armed resistance to Nazi-fascism, which escalated during the years following the September 8, 1943 armistice, and the dispersal of the Italian army, to the end of the war; and 2) the life, culture, and struggle for everyday survival of the *contadini* of the *Langhe*.[2] Fenoglio's analysis of partisan warfare and of country life, represent, in the words of Maria Corti, a *continuum narrativo*, through which Fenoglio attempts to establish a bond with his birthplace, the *Langhe*, and its people:

> I singoli innumerevoli scritti di Beppe Fenoglio vengono incontro quasi sequenze, episodi dell'impresa di un'intera vita.... Fenoglio accarezza sempre l'idea di espandere

---

[1] In this essay, I cite Fenoglio's work as *Opere* with reference to the appropriate volume.
[2] On Fenoglio's themes, see Walter Mauro (123-43).

> motivi e forme di un testo in un altro; vi è nel suo lavoro una fluidità scrittoria che assomiglia alla fluidità stessa delle fasi del vivere....
> L'attività di Fenoglio, scrittore, a parte gli abbozzi e scritti giovanili, prende l'avvio con una storia di guerra, quella partigiana, e si chiude con un'altra storia di guerra, quella mondiale: protagonista lui nella prima, un suo famigliare nella seconda. (Corti, 9-11)

In these works, Fenoglio wanted to write the history of two generations of his family, the so-called "racconti del parentado," and of the langaroli during periods of war and peace, a peace for this region and its inhabitants that Claudio Marabini describes as

> [. . .] una pace fittizia. E pace dalla guerra, ma non certo dalla povertà e dall'avverso destino: la malora, come la chiama Fenoglio. [...] Il panorama delle langhe, in cui questi racconti si ambientano, la loro cruda e fosca presenza, la loro antica vita, immutabile di sacrificio e di dolore, nutre le vicende e determina fatalmente i destini. E una battaglia continua.... (Mirabini, 571)

The primitive, almost pagan reality of life in the *Langhe*, the sense of the continuous struggle of its people, and their brutal destiny led Giovanni Orpin to paint the following portrait of the *langaroli* and, by reduction, of Fenoglio:

> Il piemontese di campagna e capace di dannarsi l'anima in Iona perpetua con una vigna arida; e con uno schioppo

> in mano può mettersi freddamente a sparare contra un carro armato tedesco: non importa la palese inferiorità, la vigna che ti imbroglia o ii carro armato che neppure si accorge dei tuoi pallini da lepre. Vuol dire che ti butterai nel pozzo, a dispetto delle viti e degli eredi, o sbatterai la testa contro le lamiere de! "Tigre." E destino, però, non "darla mai vinta" a niente e a nessuno, costi quel che ti costi alla fine. (Arpino)

Fenoglio's "testi teatrali" and the "progetto per sceneggiatura cinematografica"[3] derive from the author's above stated relationship with the *Langhe* and its people. The theatrical works, *Lo sbandato* and *Atto unico* are adapted from novels and short stories that implicitly deal with the resistance and partisan life. The film project, which would have brought the life and culture of the *Langhe* to the screen, is infused with the sense of sadness and tragedy also present in *La malora*, *Il paese*, and "i racconti del parentado," published posthumously as *Un giorno di fuoco*.[4]

---

[3] Terms used in the Einaudi edition of the *Opere*.

[4] The catalogue of the Fondo Fenoglio in Pavia contains the following information on the "progetto di sceneggiatura cinematografica":

2. Progetto di sceneggiatura cinematografica, in op. cit. 3: 419-53. Materiale dattiloscritto eterogeneo donato al Fondo da Gianfranco Bettettini. Si tratta di brani frammentari di diversa estensione e di letture autografe ruotanti attorno a un progetto di realizzazione cinematografica di argomento contadino, rimasto incompiuto, che impegno il regista Bettcttini trail 1961 e il 1962.

• Soggetto cinematografico incompleto steso su ff. 9 (mm 297 x 211) con num. d'A. datt. mg. sup. dx. recto 30-38, copie a carta carbone di originale in otto datts. solo recto, cui si aggiunge f. 1 (mm280 x 220) n.n. (num. d'ar-

Lo sbandato, a one act play with five scenes, exists in three versions, the shortest was published in the *Gazzetta del Popolo* of Torino with the title *Solitudine* just days before Fenoglio's death. The characters are "il partigiano" Sceriffo/Califfo (Fenoglio alternates the name of this character), a young seamstress, fascist soldiers, "il partigiano" Nick, a miller and his wife and townspeople. The plot unfolds during the bitter winter of 1944-1945. Califfo/Sceriffo, overcome by an oppressive feeling of solitude, decides to come out of his

---

chivio 29), datt. solo recto, di contenuto identico al .30. Tutti i ff., Sono privi di varianti. (Una copia del testo in questione con lievissime varianti, e conservata nel Fondo di Alba, cartella 13. Cfr. Nota al testo, cit., p. 734.) Al f. 32 r nota d'A. datt. mg. inf. dx. «(ti spiegherò poi la ragione di questo vuoto. E cosa di una certa imponenza».
• Sei scene dell'episodio Davide su ff.16 (mm 300 x 232) n.n. (num. d'archivio 1-16), datts. in nero, rosse didascalie e i nomi dei personaggi, solo recto senza varianti (Le sei scene recano i seguenti titoli: Morte del padre (ff. 1-3); Giocare e non giocare (ff. 4-7); Davide al mercato (scena di contrasto) (ff. 8-9); Jose si rode ma non scoppia (ff. 10-11); Josee Gino (ff. 12-14); *Il fazzoletto da testa* (ff.15-16).) Si conserva incolta: dei ff. In questione una copia carta carbone di originale ignoto con lievissime varianti, rappresentata da ff. 27 (mm 298 x 209) con num. datt. mg. sup. dx. recto 3-29 datts. solo recto 3-29 datts. solo recto.
• Quattro lettere inedite (mm 280 x 220) datts. firmate a penna sf. Blu, rispet ivamente datate: «Alba, 17 ottobre 196i»; «Alba, 26 dicembre 1961»; «Alba, 19 marzo 1962»; «Alba, 4 luglio 1962», inviate da Beppe Fenoglio a G. Bettettini e riguardanti il progetto di sceneggiatura cinematografica in questione.
Allegato al materiale autografo un tentativo di trattamento cinematografico del soggetto fenogliano ad opera di G. Bettettini su ff. 3 (mm 290 x 188) con num. d'A. ms. penna sf. blu recto e verso (solo recto il f. 1) con varianti penna sf. blu matita nera e rossa.

hiding place in the hills into the town of Benevello to see the young seamstress and spend a few hours in the company of another human being.[5] There he is discovered by a Fascist platoon and summarily executed. In the next scene we are taken inside the church where the townspeople of Benevello, the miller and Nick, who came out of his hiding place when he heard gunfire, are gathered around the casket of Sceriffo/Califfo who lies in waiting. The rest of the play focuses on the miller and Nick: The miller invites Nick to his house for dinner and then tries to convince him to come in from the hills, to hide and avoid the rest of the conflict, because, as he explains to him:

> La tua parte l'hai fatta, la tua coscienza c sicuramente a posto. E dunque smetti tutto e scendi al piano. Non per consegnarti, Dio vieti, e poi sarebbe troppo tardi. Ma scendi e un ragazzo come te, con una famiglia come la tua alle spalle, troverà certamente un nascondiglio dove stare fino alla fine della guerra, soltanto a mangiare e dormire e godersi il calduccio.

As the miller speaks, Nick quietly eats the food prepared for him, then politely rejects the advice offered and returns to the hills to await January 31, the day

---

[5] During the winter, because of the harsh conditions that made military action almost impossible, the partisan brigades would disband, and everyone would be on his own to make it through the winter and not be caught by the Nazis or the Fascists. These brigades would reassemble in the Spring to continue their guerrilla warfare.

when the partisan army is scheduled to regroup for the spring and summer campaigns.

A number of relevant similarities are revealed when one compares the three versions of the play *Lo sbandato/Solitudine* with the short story, "Nella valle di San Benedetto," written before 1952, and with the two versions of *Il partigiano Johnny*,[6] written, either during the years following the war, as Maria Corti sustains, or at a later time, 1957-59, as other critics have stated.[7] Nick is a character modeled after Johnny, the autobiographical character of *Il partigiano Johnny*. In chapter 53 of PJ1 the fascists set an ambush and kill two partisans, Ivan and Luis. As they are being buried in the town of Benevello, Johnny arrives on the scene and is asked by the town

---

[6] Fenoglio's wrote two Italian versions of *Il partigiano Johnny* and an English version, *Ur Partigiano Johnny*. I refer to these texts as PJ1, for the first version, PJ2, for the second version.

[7] The dating of these texts was the focal point of a heated intellectual debate begun in the early seventies and continued into the nineties, culminating in the volume edited by Dante Isella, *Romanzi e racconti* (Torino: Einaudi-Gallimard, 1992). Maria Antonietta Grignani, in the Nota ai testi of the second tome of the first volume of Beppe Fenoglio's *Opere*, writes the following explanatory note: "Fautrice di una datazione antica, la Corti pose come terminus ante quem per· PJl il 1949; per PJ2 partita da una datazione di poco posteriore, c giunta successivamente a con-figurare come data ante quem il 1954 (Corti 1973), mentre DeMaria su argomenti filologici cogenti già aveva indicato il prentorio teminus ante dcl periodo 1957-1958 (cfr. Anche Falaschi 1976, pp. 183-185 dove le due datazioni appaiono contraddittorie, mentre sono e possono essere complementari). I sostenitori dell'ipotesi alternativa hanno visto *Il partigiano Johnny* come prosecuzione di *"Primavera" di Bellezza*, collocabile quindi in prima redazione introno al 1956-57, in seconda stesura tra il 1958 e il 1959."

clerk for biographical data on the dead partisans. The miller of a nearby town, a friend of Johnny's, who came to Benevello expressly for the funeral, invites Johnny to his house for dinner where they plan a counter ambush. The same scene is repeated in PJ2 in the chapter titled "Inverno 7."[8] "Nella valle di San Benedetto" (*Opere* 2: 75-93) Fenoglio constructs a narrative sequence that is similar to one in the first two versions of the play: The narrator, an unnamed partisan, is thinking about what has transpired over the last few days that has brought him to his present hiding place, a tomb in a corner of the cemetery of the town of San Benedetto. After one of their numerous guerrilla actions, the narrator together with his fellow partisans, Giorgio and Bob, are trying to return home. En route they run into a column of German soldiers who open fire on them. They escape unharmed and arrive at the village of San Benedetto where they decide to go into hiding. The narrator is the only one with the courage to hide in the tomb, so he and the others part ways. After two days in hiding and with the last of his food and water gone, he suddenly hears gunfire. After all of the commotion stops, he decides it is safe to come out of hiding only to find the caskets of his two friends, Bob and Giorgio, killed by the gunfire. Besides similarities of action with the three versions of the play, this short story also delves into the mind and emotions of the protagonist: the anguish, isolation, fear, and

---

[8] For further elucidation, see Bianca de Maria.

desperation he feels while entombed among the remains of the "maestra" Enrichetta Ghirardi who died in 1928.

Atto unico, the second theatrical experiment on the partisan experience, is presented in one act with no divisions into scenes. The characters are "la signora Mussi," her daughter Lalla, and Bob, the resistance fighter. The action takes place in a "villa borghese," as the author points out to us, during the winter of 1944-45, the same time frame as *Lo sbandato/Solitudine*. It is the 20th of January, thirty-two days before the date set for the partisan fighters to regroup for the spring campaign. The play opens as Lalla's mother is writing a long letter to her sister, informing her of the events of the last year: that the village they are living in while waiting for the war to end, was a meeting place for the resistance fighters and how Lalla fell in love with Bob. She goes on to describe Bob and his family situation; he is an educated young man from a well-to-do family. At the end of this rather long narration, Bob, risking his life to see Lalla, arrives at the house, because he has something important to say, and because he desperately needs to be among people. The isolation motif seems to reoccur constantly in Fenoglio's narrative. The rest of this short play is centered on Bob and Lalla's conversation. Bob tells Lalla that he is in love with another woman, that the love he had for her was real, and that he is seeing her for the last time. He leaves and the play ends.

The reader familiar with *Una questione privata* will notice the thematic connection with that novel. In *Una questione privata* Fenoglio explores a new dimension in his saga of partisan life, and resistance literature in general: love, the private affair of the heart. In chapter thirteen of that novel Milton, Johnny's alter ego, hoping to see Fulvia, a girl with whom he had fallen in love, risks his life to return to the place where they met, a "villa borghese." She is not there, and Milton learns from the maid that Giorgio Clerici, a friend and resistance fighter, is also in love with Fulvia and that she seems to return that love. Milton decides that he must talk to Giorgio and learn the truth. Giorgio has been taken prisoner by the fascists, and the remainder of the novel follows Milton in his quest/obsession to capture a fascist officer to exchange for Giorgio in order to get an answer to his "questione privata."

A minor portion of the connective tissue that ties this "frammento fenogliano" to his epic on partisan life is the reference to the summer of 1944 when Lalla and Bob met. In the letter that Lalla's mother is writing to her sister at the beginning of the play, she states:

> ... Mi pare di averti detto nelle mie precedenti che il paese era un punto di ritrovo di tutti i partigiani delle colline circostanti. Siccome è il paese più grosso ed evoluto in tutta la valle Belbo, i partigiani ci venivano come a un Lunapark. Questo per tutta l'estate fino a buona parte di ottobre. Certe domeniche avevamo sulla piazza

> fino a cinquecento partigiani, e badogliani e comunisti.
> (*Opere* 3: 397)

Fenoglio devotes chapter thirty-three of PJ1 to describing life during the summer of 1944, which preceded the capture of Alba by the Resistance in October (*Opere* 2: 578-90). The same is true for the chapter titled "Estate" in PJ2 (*Opere* 2: 956-75).

The last work to be considered in this brief overview of Fenoglio's theatrical and cinematic texts is the "progetto di sceneggiatura cinematografica" (Opere 3: 419-53), which the author was working on in collaboration with Gianfranco Bettettini, professor of cinema at the Università di Milano and movie director. This initiative, abandoned in its initial stages due to the author's death, would have been Fenoglio's most ambitious project, second only to the writing of *Il partigiano Johnny*.

The plot of this project revolves around the vicissitudes of the Cogno's, a family of "piccoli proprietari" from San Benedetto Belbo. After the death of his father, Jose Cagno, tired of his brother's iron fisted rule, abandons the family farm and leaves the *Langhe* for Torino, where he finds work and a companion, Maria. In Torino he builds a new life but does not find happiness or fulfillment because he soon realizes that strength is bonded to the land and constantly agonizes over the problems he left behind and his share of the inheritance.

His brother Davide, on the other hand, because of his obstinate pride and intense sense of responsibility, which virtually enslaves him to the land, nurtures feelings of envy and anger toward his brother who had the courage to leave and begin a new life.

The project is divided into seven parts. In the first part, which is in narrative form, Fenoglio brings into focus the main characters of his story and sketches the plot from which the film script would be developed. Here we learn that Jose left San Benedetto Belbo to escape from the tyrannical rule of his older brother and we acquire an insight into Jose's nostalgia for his home, his wish to return, and the impossibility of it.

> Si è strappato dalla terra per pura disperazione, non sopportando più il dispotismo del fratello Davide, disgustato del lavoro in famiglia senz'altra retribuzione che il vitto. Già suo padre teneva lui, e i suoi fratelli, in questo stato servile, schiavistico-famigliare, ma morto il padre, dopo due anni di rassegnazione, non e stato più disposto a tollerare oltre dal fratello maggiore ciò che poteva tollerare dal padre.
>
> La sua nostalgia per la terra è insanabile, ma non può ritornarvi, perché sulla terra, piantatovi a gambe larghe, stava suo fratello Davide.... Maria capisce che Jose sopporta la nostalgia solo per la presenza di lei, ma capisce anche che nemmeno lei lo guarirà, nemmeno in tanti anni di quella nostalgia. (*Opere* 3: 424-25)

We read of Davide's envy of his brother because he had the courage to leave and free himself from the land. Now alone and a captive of the land, Davide's envy turns to anger:

> La defezione di Jose l'ha messo in gravissima difficolta. L'ha costretto a faticare come non mai, a farsi da solo le quattro giornate di terra, ha dovuto dimezzare le sue andate ai mercati ("a volte ti frutta più un minuto al mercato che tutta una giornata intera sudata sulla terra") ha dovuto ramazzare di lavoro anche la moglie Palma.
>
> Ma c'è dell'altro che lo monta, lo gonfia, in quelle solitarie sedute sul ciglio del rittano. Ed e l'invidia per il fratello, per il suo coraggio di strapparsi dalla terra, di togliersi dal rittano. Ha avuto, Jose, quel coraggio e ne è stato premiato: *vive*.
>
> L'invidia e il rancore per il coraggio e la fortuna di Jose gli salgono dentro, giorno per giorno. (*Opere* 3: 425-26)

We also get an insight into Maria's personality, Jose's companion, an ex-prostitute who now lives with him. The second part, titled "Davide — La morte del padre," is quite short, written in dialogue form, and deals with the event that changes their lives forever -the father's death. Part three, "Davide — giocare o non giocare," presents Jose on a typical Sunday. He wants to participate in the soccer game that is being organized but is hesitant because of his fear of losing money and then having to account for it to his brother. Frustrated, he goes to the local bar, gets caught up in a card game, and loses 200 lire. The owner of the bar tells him that it is time to stand up to this brother, that his brother has no right to make him work like a slave, and that he should not be kept impoverished. In the fourth part, Davide is in the bar on market day where he interacts with other merchants. Part V focuses on Jose's total dependency upon his older brother and his frustration and humiliation with the situation. Jose is working in front of his house when a neighboring farmer comes to discuss a business proposition with Davide. Davide is not home and Puccio, the farmer, refuses to discuss the matter with Jose:

> Puccio (reciso) —Digli che avevo un affare da proporgli. A ogni modo non è un affare che scappi. Digli che tornerò domani, e domani si faccia trovare (e fa per rigirarsi al sentiero.).
> Jose —Glielo dirò, appena torna, ma...non potete parlarne un poco con me? Puccio, almeno accennarmelo?
> Puccio (squadrandolo) —Eh? Eh, no. Perché spiegartelo a te quando debbo rispiegarlo tutto a Davide, che è l'unico che decide? Ti sembra, Jose? (*Opere* 3: 443)

Jose's humiliation is complete.

In Part VI, "Jose e Cino," it is Sunday afternoon at Placido's "osteria," and Jose is passing time watching friends playing cards. Here he sees Cino, an old friend, who left the *Langhe* to find work in Liguria. Together they go for a ride on Cino's motorcycle, and they talk about life in the city and the possibility of finding work. As their conversation progresses and he is reminded of his lot in life, his demeanor changes, and his unhappiness clearly manifests itself, "Ridiscendono. Jose non sorride più come all'andata. La faccia è tesa, gli occhi contro il vento" (*Opere* 3: 450).

In the last part of this "abbozzo" for cinema, "Il fazzoletto da testa," Jose compares his situation and that of friends. Fenoglio introduces Ettore,[9] a new character, who tells Jose that he is going to give a gift to a young lady. Jose's "sadness and depression deepen as he realizes that he cannot even have the satisfaction of giving a girl a present.[10]

Two letters written by Fenoglio to Bettettini reveal interesting insights about Fenoglio's creative process and about the thematic similarities between this work and his earlier writings on the theme of country life. In the letter dated October 17, 1961, Fenoglio states:

> Sono stato spesso sulle langhe e ho perfino intervistato langhiani interessanti, ne ho raccolto le Storie. Ho in mano tanti personaggi ed episodi ma non ho il soggetto. Avrei pronte intere sequenze di dialogo.

---

[9] For the story of Ettore, see the short story "Ettore va al lavoro," *I ventitre giorni delta città di Alba* (*Opere* 2: 315-3 3) and *La paga del sabato* (*Opere* 2: 119-23).

[10] Further narrative material about the Cogno family is published in an appendix to the "progetto di sceneggiatura cinematografica" (*Opere* 3: 734-87).

In the second letter, of March 19, 1962, Fenoglio writes: "Ho pensato al soggetto — ci penso costantemente — e ne ho studiato uno che però è da abbandonare. Troppo truculento. Finisce con un fratricidio." Fenoglio is referring to the plot of "Ferragosto" (*Opere* 2: 589-99) from the so-called "racconti del parentado," published with the collective title of *Un giorno di fuoco* (*Opere* 2: 437-607). Toni, a "langarolo inurbato" returns home with the woman he is going to marry, a former prostitute. Pietro, the brother, refuses to allow her to enter the house, calling her the "porcheria della grande città." This precipitates a fight that ends with Toni being brutally killed by his brother: "gli arrivò dietro con un'accetta e da dietro gliela calò sulla testa spaccandogliela come una noce" (*Opere* 2: 599).

Although Fenoglio decides against the ending of "Ferragosto" for his film project, it is hard to imagine that this film would have been blessed with a happy ending. In this late stage of his life, Fenoglio is totally detached from his material as he proceeds thematically and formally toward a representation of reality that is anything but optimistic.

When taken together, the theatrical works and the "progetto di sceneggiatura cinematografico" are connected by a continuously recurring leitmotif in Fenoglio's art, solitude. This element, more than similarities in action and plot lines, ties Fenoglio's work together and is what Maria Corti meant by her phrase "continuum narrativo." This existential reality rendered explicit by Sceriffo in *Solitudine*:

> Non resisto più. Più. Ora mi muovo. Ma che posso fare, Dove voglio andare? non resisto più. Col freddo e con la fame posso ancora dirla, ma alla solitudine non ci resisto più. Debbo veder gente. (alza la voce). Voglio veder gente. (*Opere* 3: 380-81)

When Sceriffo decides that he must have contact with other human beings, he determines his own fate.

In Atto Unico that same oppressive sentiment of solitude permeates Bob's words to Lalla:

> Bob -Ma chi ci arriva al trentuno?
> Lalla-Bob?
> Bob —Bada che non parlo di morire. Parlo d'impazzire. Perché io, Lalla, impazzisco. Perché non sono nel mio elemento, perché non mi ci trovo. Perché mi ci sperdo. (ribalza in piedi, ma non si aggira) Sento delle nausee. La collina mi fa nausea, il cielo mi fa nausea, tutto mi fa nausea, le strade mi fanno nausea. Per esempio, a solo pensare al ritorno, adesso, io sono già pazzo. (*Opere* 3: 413-14)

He continues by describing the loneliness of life in the hills while hiding or waiting for the next battle:

> E così tu te ne esci alle tre, nel cuore della notte, nel pieno del freddo, nel caos del mondo. Non sai che fare, non hai dove andare, se non muoverti per reagire al freddo.

> Ti muovi per i boschi, per i sentieri, come... come un'anima a cui non sia stato assegnato niente, né il paradiso né l'inferno e nemmeno il purgatorio. (*Opere* 3: 415)

This sense of extreme, almost wrenching, solitude and isolation is a central motif of Fenoglio's writing and is palpably present in almost all the pages of his novels and short stories. The following excerpt from P]l speak to this existential condition with a clarity that needs no explanation:

> D'un tratto, nell'ombra franante, ebbe il raggelante sogno di trovarsi lui solo in quella posizione, un solitario fuorilegge, autobanditosi per motivi non chiari nemmeno a lui stesso, precisatisi in un incubo e che ora si trovasse, solo, di fronte a tutto un mondo inferocito e vendicativo.
> ... li hanno uccisi. Io sono vivo. Ma sono vivo? Sono solo, solo, solo e tutto è finito.

Solitude and isolation are Milton's only companions as he searches the *Langhe* for a fascist officer to capture and exchange for Giorgio, and as he runs away from the fascists and their bullets at the end of the novel:

> Correva ancora, ma senza contatto con la terra corpo, movimenti, respiro, fatica, vanificati.... Ma i pensieri venivano dal di fuori come ciottoli scagliati da una fionda. "Sono vivo. Fulvia, sono solo. Fulvia, a momenti mi ammazzi!" (*Opere* 1.3: 2062)

Solitude and isolation are also present in the last paragraph of the novel that describes Milton's last moments:

> Correva, con gli occhi sgranati, vedendo pochissimo della terra e nulla del cielo. Era perfettamente conscio della solitudine, del silenzio, della pace, ma ancora correva, facilmente, irresistibilmente. Poi gli si parò davanti un bosco e Milton vi puntò dritto. Come entro sotto gli alberi, questi parvero serrare e far muro e a un metro da quel muro crollo. (*Opere* 1.3: 2063)

The same is true for the protagonists of the "progetto di sceneggiatura cinematografica," "Ferragosto," and the other novels and short stories that speak of life in the *Langhe*. Solitude and isolation drive Jose to leave his home, they are Agostino's companions as he leaves his home to work as a hired hand in the short novel *La malora* and take away Superino's hope and push him to drown himself in the river Belbo in the homonymous short story (*Opere* 2: 487-505).

All Fenoglio's work confirms a realistic human condition that is emblematic of a world dominated by the tragic necessity of violence and loneliness. Fenoglio's universe is populated with characters that are "vinti." The people who inhabit Fenoglio's world are overwhelmed by historical events, economic conditions and a land, the *Langhe*, that will always take more than it will give back. Fenoglio's partigiani and the fascists of Salò are not central characters on the world stage, but at best marginal.[11] His *contadini* fight a continuous battle against poverty, prejudice, tradition and the elements; a battle they are not destined to win. In a short story, discovered in the Fondo Fenoglio, which bears no title, two resistance fighters meet one day years after the end of the war. The two reminisce and address each other by their partisan names, Nick and Jimmy. The short story ends as "Nick/Fenoglio ... pensò. —Mi chiamava *old lion* con convinzione. Eppure, se n'è accorto, sicurissimamente, che sono un fallimento" (*Opere* 3: 124).

References

Arpino, Giovanni. "Un piemontese di campagna," *Il giorno*, 1 June 19.

Corti, Maria. *Beppe Fenoglio storia di un "continuum narrativo"*. Padova: Liviana Editrice, 1980.

De Maria, Bianca. "Le due redazioni del Partigiano Johnny: rapporti interni e datazione," *Nuovi argomenti* 35-36 (1973): 132-67.

---

[11] David Ward, in his book *Antifascisms: Cultural Politics in Italy, 1943-46*, makes an interesting statement on the Resistance struggle and what prompted men and women to play a part in this struggle: "But what of the broader Resistance struggle for national liberation, against whose background Milton plays out his private quest? In a manner that certainly met with Calvino's approval, Fenoglio suggests the Resistance struggle itself acts as a pretext for another struggle, this one located at a deeper, more personal, and irrational level.... Men and women, Fenoglio suggests, do not put their lives at risk for abstract historical goals like national liberation. Only when historical goals march to the same beat as those individual aspirations and desires that are located in the private recesses of their psychological make-up will men and women be willing to die for a cause" (122-23).

Mauro, Walter. *Invito alla lettura di Fenoglio*, 3rd ed. Milano: Mursia, 1976.
Marabini, Claudio. "Fenoglio," *Nuovi argomenti* 510 (1970): 5
Ward, David. *Antifascisms: Cultural Politics in Italy*. Madison, NJ: Fairleigh Dickinson UP, 1996.

Part III

Translation

"The Victim"

Bernardino Ciambelli

On that October morning the vast reception room of the Barge Office, where the newly arrived file past the visual control of the Immigration Agents, was extremely crowded; the transatlantic steamers had brought more than two thousand immigrants from Europe, some were German, some were Russian Jews, but most came from the Southern regions of Italy.

The Jews, with their cautious demeanor, buttoned up in their long shabby coats all trimmed with fur, formed a group apart from the others, as though they were afraid to mingle with the crowd that swarmed around them. The Germans, serious but satisfied, like those that arrive in a conquered land, remained close to one another like soldiers ready to attack the enemy. The Italian, happy, non-caring, loud, were a cheerful note to the group, giving it life with their observations, spoken in loud voices in the various dialects of the Southern provinces, that flow from a barbaric accent to the softness of the Arab tongue.

The immigrants filed one by one, to be interrogated, as was the custom, by the Immigration Agents. More than half of the immigrants had passed, when, from the Italian group, a beautiful young woman came forth, whose dress and manner were nothing like those of her travel mates. In fact, while the immigrant women flaunted showy colored dresses, cloths and shawls, dominated by reds, yellows and greens, the woman that was passing in front of the agents was dressed in elegant simplicity; a black skirt, non-new but clean, enveloped her elegant moving body, a waistcoat, also black, imprisoned her supple waist and her full and provocative bosom; a small round hat of the same color covered her head. Her beautiful Hellenic face, framed by her luxurious black hair, was left completely uncovered.

The woman's eyes, two large deep blue almond shaped eyes, with a sweet and kind expression, veiled by long eyelashes, flitted back and forth, timid and fearful; but when they rested on the sweet child that she held by the hand, they took on such a loving expression, that showed how much that beautiful immigrant woman loved and adored that child, who must have been her son, because only mothers can show such affection in their eyes.

The woman found herself in front of the agent. The civil servant looked at her surprised, and changing the brusque and rough tone that he customarily used, began the usual interrogations; realizing that the woman was Italian he called the interpreter and had him ask her the questions:

"What is your name?"

"Vittoria Ruiz," the woman answered with a sweet and melodious voice.

"Where do you come from?"

"From Naples."

"Is this your son?"

"Yes" she answered with a certain pride.

"Do you have relatives in New York?"

Vittoria hesitated a moment and then resolutely answered:

"Yes, my husband!"

"Enough, you can pass."

Vittoria Ruiz started for the door, she did not understand the money changers who were yelling in her ears if she had money to exchange, she did not hear the hotel agents that offered their services, she walked straight towards the door, as if she was in a hurry to touch the pavement of the biggest Metropolis of the American Union. She did not even stop to say goodbye to her travel companions, nor did she see the longing gaze of a young man, who, lost among the immigrants, looked at her with great veneration.

When the woman found herself outside the Barge Office, her bosom rose, breathless, and a sigh escaped her lips along with this word: "Finally!"

II THE DEMON

The fog enveloped Battery Place; the towers of the Barge Office were lost in the dark and gloomy smog and the coast of the river had disappeared, as if a large curtain had been spread out in front of her, the foghorns of the steam ships sounded their mournful song.

Vittoria Ruiz, from now on we will call her by the name she gave to the immigration agents, stood for a moment on the threshold of the Barge Room, she looked at the fog that was becoming thicker and then took her first steps into the unknown. The boy, afraid, held on tight to his mother's skirt, who, with a steady pace, started down one of the many avenues that cut across Battery Place. Where was she headed? The poor woman had no idea!

All of a sudden, as she was entering State Street, she felt a hand on her shoulder, while a caressing voice said to her in English: "Well, my dear, where are you going?" Vittoria turned, startled and afraid. But seeing in front of her a woman with gray hair with a sweet demeanor, she felt reassured and using gestures made the lady understand that she did not understand the language that was being spoken to her. The old woman understood. Immediately and with great haste she said, this time in Italian.

"Did you arrive from Naples?"

Vittoria hearing the language of her land felt a thrill of joy and answered: "Yes, I come from Naples."

"Well then, we are fellow countrywomen." The old woman replied.

Vittoria did not notice that though the woman spoke Italian she did so with a very pronounced accent, she was just happy to have found a person from her country; she held out her hand innocently, a hand that could have belonged to a duchess.

"And why did we come to America, my sweet dove?" She continued in an insinuating way.

"That is my secret, and I will not tell it to anyone."

"Keep your secret; the child, is he your son?"

"Yes, he is my dear Enrico."

"But tell me, where are you headed?"

"I don't know."

"You don't know? Do you have anyone in New York?

Vittoria hesitated and then answered: "No one!"

"Money. Do you have any?"

"No, Everything I had went for passage on the steamer."

A flash of joy lit up the old woman's face, and for a moment took on a look of disgust.

"My dear girl, you were born under a lucky star," the old woman said. "I am looking for a girl to be a companion to a fine, rich Italian lady, and if you do not have any objections....

"Ah! My dear lady, you are my savior. It is God who has sent you.

The old woman smiled maliciously, she certainly thought that it wasn't God that had sent her at that time.

"So, you accept?"

"With all my heart."

"But there is one problem. The lady for whom you will become chaperone is on vacation and won't return until mid-November."

"Oh my God, where will I stay until then?"

"That's a good one! You will stay with me, my house is not really nice, but for a short time it will do. You'll see, from my house one is often and eagerly drawn to go and live in a beautiful villa, all trimmed in lace . . . that's enough, we'll see if you are reasonable; let's be on our way.

Vittoria, her new companion and the child set out towards the center of the City. The fog continued to get thicker. In that smog the people lost their forms and began to look like shadows.

III V̲ittoria R̲uiz

Before we continue, we will tell you why Vittoria Ruiz and her child landed in New York on the morning of October 15, 1891.

Vittoria was a member of an honest and respectable family of Naples, and until the age of twelve she had lived in comfort, adored by her father, a rich businessman who was loved and esteemed by everyone; her mother died giving birth to her. One morning the poor child found herself in front of the body of her father, who had committed suicide to escape from a disastrous business failure. The young girl almost died from grief, and for two months lived in a state of madness. When she began to remember, she was told that to live she had to work. She began working in a milliner's shop in Via Toledo for her room and board.

Vittoria was already a woman at the age of fourteen, and her beauty attracted the stares of all that saw her. More than one dandy became a frequent visitor of the store where Vittoria worked. But it was all in vain, because the young girl didn't seem to notice them.

One day though her heart throbbed, love broke the ice that enveloped her and made her understand that it is man's destiny to love and to be loved. It was the day of the feast of the altars at Torre del Greco that Vitoria met for the first time the man that would eventually make her shed so many tears. Her mistress, like a good Neapolitan, had gone to admire the famous flower rugs, genuine exquisite mosaics made by the people of Torre del Greco, and had taken Vittoria along. During the evening, while the music played in the piazza, and the fireworks turned the dark sky into a magical tapestry of lights, a wayward rocket hit her clothes made of light muslin and her dress immediately caught fire.

A cry of terror escaped the lips of the frightened child as the crowd looked on, paralyzed. The flames were beginning to burn her flesh when a young man hurled himself on her, held her in his arms and, at the risk of burning himself, smothered the flames.

The crowd enthusiastically applauded the young man. Vittoria fainted. When she came to, she saw the young courageous man at her side, held out her hand and whispered, "Thank you!" The girl's rescuer must have been twenty years old, elegant, slender, with a head of black hair that made his pale complexion stand out; he had all the physical qualities to be proclaimed a handsome young man; only his eyes, his beautiful eyes, had a steel and sinister gaze; it was an evil look.

His name was Rinaldo Ruiz. His parents, who had been dead for a while, were Spanish. He lived a comfortable life in Naples without anyone knowing precisely where his resources came from. Some whispered that he was the kept man of an old rich lady, others said he was a gambler, while others ventured that the well-dressed young man, of aristocratic manner was a notorious thief. Was there any truth in all the gossip? Maybe Rinaldo Ruiz was all those things, a kept man, a gambler and a thief. Vittoria fell completely and madly in love with her savior; the warnings of her mistress, the supplications of close friends that begged her not to tie her future to an unworthy man, had the reverse effect. Instead of diminishing, her passion for the young man grew.

Ruiz, proud to be the by the most beautiful young woman of the neighborhood, hung around the shop where Vittoria worked and tried to make her his lover, but the girl resisted and kept her honor intact. Ruiz, excited by her resistance to his advances, and wanting to possess at all costs the beautiful virgin, gave in and married Vittoria.

The first three months of matrimony were, for the young lady, who was only fifteen years old, a dream of constant joy and happiness that words could never explain. Ruiz rented a small, beautiful apartment in the neighborhood of "Largo della Carità" where the young married couple lived a comfortable life. Vittoria's happiness did not last long. Her husband soon began to stay out all night, and when he returned home, he was drunk more often than not. It was during those times that he would experience horrid hallucinations that terrified him and react with violent outbursts. One evening, the same day Vittorias learned that she was pregnant, Ruiz returned home in a horrible state, his clothes were ripped, and he was covered in blood and mud.

"I came to change my clothes and pack some underwear because I have to go to Avellino."

When his wife asked him why he was reduced to such a state and where did all that blood come from, he answered in a trembling voice that he came to aid of a painter friend who had fallen from abridge he was working on. Ruiz quickly packed his suitcase, changed his clothes, and without saying a word abandoned his home. That night and the next and the following nights Vittoria waited in vain for her husband's return.

Two days after that awful evening, Vittoria read in the "Corriere di Napoli" the horrible details of the murder of a rich banker, who, drawn into a deserted house near Posillipo, certainly by a pretty woman, was killed and robbed; the police found the body but there were no clues that could lead to the identity of the assassins.

Vittoria, in reading that bit of news, had e premonition that Ruiz, her husband, the father of the child growing in her womb was one of the authors of that crime, and was overwhelmed by a great fear. Soon, not having money to pay the rent she had to leave the apartment she was living in, and with the money she made from selling her furniture, about 600 lire, she furnished a small room in Pigna Secca and returned to work at the milliner's shop. Almost a year to the day that Vittoria met Ruiz she gave birth to a son, on whom she concentrated all her love.

Five years passed without any news of her husband; one day, two months before our novel begins, a woman who had just arrived from America, met Vittoria and told her:

"I saw your husband in New York, he is a gentleman with class and demeanor, he pisses away money big time, and I believe that he is ready to take another wife."

"Are you really certain of what you are telling me?"

"Certain as I am certain that S. Gennaro is the patron Saint of Naples."

Vittoria immediately decided. She wanted to find the man who had so cowardly abandoned her. She sold the furniture and all her belongings, and, with her child, boarded a steamship of the "Fabre Line and sailed for New York.

During the long crossing she kept herself separate from the other passengers. Completely absorbed by her grief she barely noticed the disgusting filth that surrounded her. Being of a delicate nature she tolerated, without noticing it, repugnant contacts, and only reacted when some bold lout dared speak to her in a manner that was less than respectful.

From the beginning, the passengers dubbed her "Madonnina" and were very attentive to her needs. But Vittoria occupied by other thoughts, didn't notice their attention and kindness, so they began calling her the proud one and left her alone as if she had the plague. Only one passenger, a good-looking young man with an honest face, who conducted himself with distinction, developed a great admiration and affection for the poor soul; but he never showed his feelings, well understanding that the beautiful woman was prey to a grief and sorrow that would be impossible to console.

After 18 days at sea the "Neustria" arrived in New York. Vittoria set foot on American soil, where more misfortune and evil awaited her.

IV IN THE LAIR

Vittoria had come to America without even thinking about the dangers that she might be faced with. Her burning desire to find her husband so occupied her thoughts and directed her actions that it did not even cross her mind that arriving in an unknown foreign place, without money, without friends, without any support would certainly lead to a series of terrible disasters.

The woman, that chance brought her for a companion from the moment she set foot on dry land, seemed to the poor thing a blessing from Providence, so she followed her with joy, not suspecting for a moment what birds of prey await the poor immigrants when they arrive.

Vittoria and her son followed the unknown woman across Battery Place, a part of State Street and found herself on Broadway, the main avenue of New

York. In the meantime, neither the immigrant, nor her companion were aware that a young man, the same one we saw in the great waiting hall of the Barge Office, followed their footsteps; The sidewalks of Broadway were so crowded that the young man didn't stand out.

The bells rang noon and from the majestic office buildings a sea of employees swarmed forth, quickly going to the beer halls, the "Lunchrooms", and the bakeries for their lunch. On Broadway the fog was lighter and more transparent. Vittoria glimpsed, as if in a dream, at the upscale stores where the electric lights glowed while barely hearing the voice of her companion, who, at every chance, repeated: "If one uses good judgment, one can attain anything one wants in New York." The young Enrico, shuffled behind his mother, hanging on to her clothes, afraid of losing her. The old woman held out her hand to him, but he did not want to hold it at any cost. After they crossed the plaza of City Hall, the woman guided Vittoria through Centre Street and then Worth Street, Paradise and Park Street, ending up at Mulberry Street. The fog had cleared and the sun, red like a brass disc, hung over the city giving it an aura of sadness and fear.

When she set foot in Mulberry Street Vittoria looked around dumbfounded, as though she had just wakened from a long deep sleep. That street reminded her of one the streets of her beautiful city where she was born; it reminded her of one of the working-class neighborhoods of her beloved Naples, and for a moment thought that the trip and the arrival in America were nothing more than a dream that had lasted a long time. Around her she heard the picturesque dialect of her city, she saw types, figures seen other times when she, happy and careless, walked through the streets and avenues of Naples. Her companion brought her back to reality, telling her rudely that it was necessary to walk faster and get home because her man would go into a beastly rage when he didn't find lunch ready and on the table by noon.

Vittoria automatically followed the woman, happy to find so many things that reminded her of her native land.

"Here we are, my lovely." The old woman said suddenly, "It's not a palace but we have to be satisfied."

It definitely wasn't a palace, it was a low two-story house, the front was the color of clotted blood, blackish, and had the appearance of a hovel; on the ground floor there were two shops with dirty windows, broken in a number of places and repaired with paper of an indefinable color. Under the shops a hollow that lead to the cellar where a crude sign announced, "Italian Restaurant, Maccheroni with Tomato Sauce."

Vittoria and her guide entered a narrow open corridor between two houses into a small courtyard crammed with debris, where a dirty rivulet spread its filthy waters everywhere, making the uneven stone pavement slippery. At the back of the courtyard, a rickety old door led to a ramshackle staircase, where a greasy rope, slimy like the skin of a snake, served to support those that went up and down those unstable stairs.

"Follow me, don't be afraid, my beauty." The old woman said to Vittoria, "In this neighborhood we don't have staircases and courtyards made from marble."

Despite her disgust for the filth that surrounded her, the resolute young woman made for the stairs. When they arrived on the second floor, the woman knocked on the door; a grunt, not resembling anything human, answered, followed by staggering steps. Finally, the door opened.

"Damn... whore! You're finally home," he yelled in pure French.

"Shut up stupid, I'm with good company," Vittoria's companion answered in the same language.

"Good company, what do I care!"

"You're drunk again! You brute! Get out of the way and the let this beautiful lady with me pass!"

"A lady? I understand. Make way for the ladies, as we used to say in Belleville in the good old days."

The drunk barely finished his sentence when his wife pushed him and sent him rolling to the middle of the room.

"Come in without fear, my beauty, that animal drank too much today and doesn't know what he's saying."

That disgusting scene left a vivid impression on Vittoria. The woman to whom she had blindly entrusted herself and her son to did not seem good and honest. Not knowing French, she did not understand the words exchanged by the couple, but by the tone in which they were said she understood that it involved some sort of threat. Nonetheless, she entered that small room with the smoke blackened ceiling that must have served as kitchen, dining room, and even as a bedroom, because there was a cot in the corner with dirty linens and a torn pillow that spilled its cotton stuffing from its numerous wounds.

On the cast iron stove, in a tin saucepan a sauce made from onion was cooking, emitting an acrid, sharp, nauseating smell that stuck in poor Vittoria's throat, making it impossible for her not to show her disgust. An expression that did not go unnoticed by her protector, who quickly tried to reassure her by saying:

"Don't worry, we are not going to eat that stuff."

"You're not going to eat." yelled the drunken man who had lifted himself from the floor, "This sauce is a nectar, you'll see my sweet princess." While saying this he approached Vittoria and held out his filthy hand to caress her chin.

The young lady pulled back with a shudder, that man disgusted her. Indeed, it wasn't possible to have a more repugnant face than his. His eyes were small, yellow, and phosphorescent; the cheeks purulent and scrofulous; the nose, a living red, resembled an armor of disgusting scabs; a thin mustache with bald spots, shaded his big lips, turned inside out, sinuous, and disfigured on the sides by ulcerous sores.

"I don't want to eat you," grumbled the monster, seeing the look of disgust that came from Vittoria.

"Napoleon, that's enough," thundered the old woman, "leave the child alone, and heaven help you if you dare touch a hair on her head."

Vittoria looked at the old woman with gratitude, who whispered to her: "He isn't bad, my Napoleon, but today he drank a bit more than usual." The young Enrico was deathly afraid of Napoleon and hid in his mother's dress.

"Now, my girl, we are safe and surely you both need to rest, we'll talk business after we eat, and you will see that the devil is not as ugly as he is painted."

"No, he is beautiful, beautiful like ... me," grumbled Napoleon.

"Here you will live like a small queen," continued the woman, not paying any attention to her husband's interruption, "we will give you the best room, we are not as poor as you may think. Look, here is your apartment." She opened a door and pushed Vittoria into a charming room, wallpapered in light blue with gold stars, with an elegant carpet designed with bunches of violets on the floor, and a large bed made from carved walnut, and chairs covered with deep blue velvet.

An oil lamp, with a porcelain bell and crystal pendants, illuminated the room. Vittoria was amazed by the sudden change. On the other side of the threshold, misery, filth, negligence, here elegance, luxury, almost wealth. The old woman saw the astonishment on the young woman's face. And quickly said: "This is the custom in this country, neglect everything to beautifully furnish one room.

"But I can't allow you to deprive yourself of your comfort for me!"

"Don't say it even as a joke, Mamma Margherita knows the duties of a host, and then, after you've settled yourself, you will repay me. Now rest, then we will have a good meal and discuss our business, goodbye, my beauty, and think of this as your house."

Vittoria took one of Margherita's hands, brought it with veneration to her lips and whispered, "Thank you."

The old woman had an evil smile on her lips as she left, leaving the young immigrant woman alone.

Vittoria fell to her knees and thanked God for having sent her someone who would protect her. The poor thing still did not understand that she had fallen into the most heinous trap.

V. Traffickers in Human Flesh

As soon as mamma Margherita found herself alone with her worthy husband, in a stifled voice she uttered:

"The bird is in the cage; it is beautiful and who wants to buy it will have to pay dearly. Spread the word in the usual places you know, speak of it to that half Spanish half Italian merchant you're acquainted with. You know what a libertine he is and how generous. If we do this right, we could have a real gold mine on our hands.

"You're right the little one is pretty enough, but I..."

"Silence, animal, she is not stuff for your teeth."

"What about the child, wife of mine?"

"Your question tells me that you've sobered up; in time the boy will disappear, but if the beautiful immigrant knows what is wanted from her, she can keep him, if she becomes fussy and hard to please, then we'll see. Now don't waste time, go to the shopkeeper Ruizzi and inform him of my beautiful catch. As soon as he smells fresh meat, he runs like a hyena when he is hungry."

"I'll go but first let me eat my onion stew."

In what hands had the bride Ruiz fallen into?

The unfortunate woman had the bad luck of bumping into one of those miserable human beings that hang around the Barge Office, waiting for some poor young lady, alone from Europe, who can be tempted by seductive words, and taken to wicked places where she ends up disgraced.

These hags, who the police see but do not disturb because they pay them a good sum of money in bribes to be able to practice their despicable profession. They lure these poor naïve creatures with a thousand promises. Respectable in appearance, they deceive even those that are on their guard, and will do anything, with force or love, to make these young ladies available to degenerates, young and old, who, to slake their lust, pay these traffickers of human flesh handsomely.

Mamma Margherita was one of these women, and one of the most dangerous. She was highly thought of in the world of the pleasure seekers because she had done some masterful things, and in that small room wallpapered in blue, in her house on Mulberry, more than one poor girl had lost her innocence, and taken the first step on that slippery road that leads to a brothel, prison, and eventually the hospital.

Margherita and Napoleon passed themselves off as Mr. and Mrs. Gherardini from Naples. Their name and country were false, their name was really Gautier, and they came from Marseille.

Margherita had spent her youth in the small wine bars that you find everywhere along the dirty alleys in the vicinity of the New Port of Marseille, where sailors go to appease their lust after their long voyages. Corrupt in body and soul, shrewd and clever, at the age of sixteen Margherita negotiated her body like a Jewish merchant negotiates his merchandise. She earned lots of money but it did not remain long in her pockets; Napoleon Gautier, a member of that revolting breed that in Marseille they called "nervi", he was Margherita's idol and all the money the wretched woman made went to him. At the age of 25, worn-out and old before her time, Margherita became Gautier's wife and at the same time the proprietor of the popular 100 Rue Bellegarde that the refined world of Marseille and the surrounding area knew well. For a while business was quite good, but when the police discovered that at 100 Rue Bellegarde underage young girls were being sold, they ordered the arrest of the Gautier's. Tipped off by some of their high-ranking customers, the Gautiers took flight and went to Italy.

In Marseille, the quintessential cosmopolitan city, all languages are spoken but particularly Italian. Margherita and Napoleon spoke this language well, so when they decided to go to America, they changed their name and in New York they passed themselves off as Italians and went to live in that quintessential Italian neighborhood – Mulberry.

In America they continued their old work and made out quite well. Whenever a steamboat arrived, Margherita ran to the Barge Office and, when she thought the moment was right, she would spread her net and heaven help who was caught in the trap. More than once on Mulberry you would hear of the heinous work of the Gautiers but nothing certain could ever be said because they were very careful and took all precautions. Anyway, they were rich and with money all crimes can be easily covered up.

This is the situation the poor wretch Vittoria Ruiz had fallen into, and the dangers that threatened her.

VI. *The Lover*

The young man that had followed Vittoria from the Barge Office, followed her to Mulberry, and firmly engraved in his mind the place where the woman, that had awakened in his heart the most powerful love, had entered.

The house did not have a number, but the young lover would have found it even in the darkest night. This young man, who by all indications did fit the mold of your usual immigrant, was named Alberto Righetti. He was from a noble Florentine family and had emigrated to America seduced by visions of gold that the land discovered by Columbus promised.

Alberto Righetti educated, cultured, and well-mannered would quickly realize that America is not a place for those that are not adapt to manual labor and do not have a trade. Alberto saw Vittoria on board of the "Neustria" and was immediately struck by her beauty. During the voyage he often saw her sad and melancholy, and more than once he tried to console her but to no end, Vittoria would turn her back to him without saying a word. Alberto suffered from her rejection; he suffered cruelly for not being able to alleviate the pain of the woman he had fallen in love with.

When the steamship arrived in New York, Alberto offered his services to Vittoria. She thanked him but formally declared that she did not need anyone's help. We then saw him follow the young mother to Mulberry where the honor and life of Vittoria were in the greatest of danger.

VII. *The Contract*

Napoleon Gherardini, after having eaten his onion stew, put on a long black overcoat, which had turned a shiny dark red over the years, and hurried to the office of the wholesaler Ruizzi, to whom he revealed the news, in the strictest of confidence, that a morsel fit for a king was awaiting at his house, and that if he desired to sample it he was the preferred one.

The wholesaler had greeted the happy news with great satisfaction, saying that if the bird was worth it, he would not skimp on the price.

"This is a rare bird," said Napoleon, "but it is necessary to wait until it's more domesticated."

"OK, you'll tell me when the time is right," added the libertine.

Rinaldo Ruizzi was young, he could not have been more than 26. The women found him handsome. His hair, his eyes were black like ebony, and the paleness of his skin highlighted his features, that were spoiled his stare; cold, evil, and inflexible like the blade of a dagger.

Ruizzi had been in America only five years and he had already made quite a position for himself.

His store of Venetian glass was a gold mine, and the number of clients grew by the day. Bold, entrepreneurial, he seized fortune by the horns, and everything was going well for him.

No one knew exactly where he came from, and he was very careful not to let anyone know.

Every once and awhile, the word on the street, immediately stifled, was that the merchants name was not Ruizzi, and that he wasn't even Italian. But there was no proof to the gossip. The handsome Rinaldo was held in high esteem by everyone, and he brilliantly continued his career, thirsty for good times, orgies and pleasure.

Margherita was one of Ruizzi's suppliers, money being of no concern when she brought him "a pretty little thing."

Let's imagine then how Ruizzi anxiously awaited a call from the Gherardini's, a call that meant a night of infinite sweetness in the arms of a naïve woman who had fallen in the clutches of Margherita.

VIII. *THE FIRST SIGNS*

Three days went by. This was all the time Margherita needed to learn why Vittoria came to New York.

Vittoria's disclosures about her life had dissolved all apprehensions that trafficker of human flesh might have had. Really, what did she have to fear?

Vittoria didn't know the name her husband was known by in America; she had left Naples without knowing the identity of the woman that brought her the news of her husband so she could find her and ask her more precise questions. The unfortunate woman had given in to a moment of elation, and she believed that once in New York everyone would have been able to tell her where he lived. The old Margherita did not discourage Vittoria; on the contrary, she made her understand that with her help it would be easy to know where Ruiz lived. In the meantime, the shrewd woman began to test the waters and slowly turned the conversation to the unexpected adventures that happened to many young girls who were able to latch on to that unstable Goddess, fortune.

Vittoria, sweet innocent soul that she was, listened in awe, like a child that listen to the tales of the *One Thousand and One Nights,* to what her protectress said, and not once did she think about what price the conquest of wealth cost those beautiful girls.

Vittoria lived in that depressing house on Mulberry like a prisoner, and from the day she arrived she had not gone outside. She didn't even look out the window because Margherita had told her that for her own good, she should not be seen by the neighbors, who, being gossipy and blabbermouths, would have told the whole neighborhood about her arrival and possibly cause her an infinity of problems and grief.

Occasionally, she would hear the echo of a festive Neapolitan song, sung full blast by happy people who lived near the Ghirendini and who did not have the faintest idea of the drama that was unfolding right next to them. From the window of Margherita's filthy kitchen, Vittoria saw, through the balcony of the house across the way, a young bride, beautiful, with fresh complexion, in total bliss, admiring the beautiful child she held in her arms to whom she offered in total grace her breast that was full of milk. Vittoria looked on the scene deeply moved and would have given anything to embrace that chubby rosy cheeked child. On the fourth day of her imprisonment, Vittoria had a moment of freedom. Seeing the woman and the child, she opened the window, and yelled:

"What a dear beautiful child!"

The happy mother raised her radiant gaze from her child and thanked the beautiful lady, who, by praising her son, had conquered her affection. Vittoria, hearing the young mother speaking with a strong southern accent, asked her with glee:

"Are you Neapolitan?"

"From Potenza. Have you just arrived from Italy?"

"Yes." Victoria answered.

"Who are you staying with?"

"In the home of a kind woman who has offered me her hospitality."

"Are you staying at the Gherardini's?"

"Yes."

"Be careful and keep your guard up, my dear."

"Be careful, why?"

She couldn't say more. Margherita entered the house and pulled her violently from the window, "Are you crazy?" she yelled at her in a gruff voice.

Vittoria, taken aback by Margherita's violent reaction, did not have the strength to utter a word, but, from that moment she was possessed by a vague fear, her sense of security had vanished, and she promised herself to follow the advice that was just given her and to be on her guard.

In the evening of that same day that had left such an impression on Vittoria, the witch began to show her cards. Supper had ended. Napoleon was already snoring away like a double bass in a corner of the small living room, his face, red from too many libations, was more horrible than ever. The young Enrico had fallen asleep with his head on his mother's knee. In a sweet, honeyed voice, Margherita began:

"My dear girl, as hard as I have searched, it has been impossible to find any trace of your husband; New York is big, and one cannot do in a few days what is quite easy to do in a small town. You now also have to think about yourself. The woman I had spoken to you about doesn't need a maid anymore, so it is necessary to look elsewhere."

"You are absolutely right, it's necessary that I work, I can't continue to be in your debt."

"I'm not saying this because of that, my angel; what I'm saying is in your best interest, and if you heed what I say, you will be better off for it."

"Dear lady, I will listen to you, as I listened to my poor mother."

"Good! Now listen up. In America people are not as scrupulous as we are in Italy, one comes here to make money, then we go back to our towns and no one thinks about asking you how, where, and in what manner you accumulated your fortune. I know ladies that in Europe are thought of as Gran Dames, while here they did all sorts of things."

A great fear crept over poor Vittoria as she listened to those strange words, and, though she wanted to better understand the soul of this woman who was beginning to show her true face, she did not say a word to interrupt her. Margherita, corrupt, wicked, and not capable of understanding the real meaning of Vittoria's silence, understood it as a tacit agreement, and began to freely give vent to her talk.

"You," continued the old woman, "don't owe anything to your husband. He abandoned you and you should consider him dead. Now, widowhood cannot be eternal, you're beautiful, quite beautiful, and more than one man, I am sure, would be pleased to possess you. . . Listen, I know many Italian gentlemen, you could choose one that would console you and at the same time avenge the treachery of your husband's desertion.

The mask had completely vanished, Vittoria now had no more doubts that the woman that Vittoria had believed to be her protector sent from heaven, wanted her ruined. She still did not know that they wanted sell her body, but she understood that they wanted to throw her in the arms of some man. Her sense of feminine decency rebelled, she proudly lifted her head and with a resolute voice said:

"I don't know what the purpose of this conversation is but understand that I have been and will remain faithful to my husband. If I don't find him, I will work and earn enough for me and my son to live on. I'm not afraid."

"But..." the old woman began.

"Enough on this subject, if not I will leave this house immediately."

Margherita understood. It was useless to insist, and not wanting to lose her victim changed her tactic and said:

"I approve of your pride. I didn't want to suggest anything dishonest; I was only referring to a possible husband who would make you rich and happy. This is not for you. We won't talk about it anymore, finished.

"Dear lady, tomorrow I will begin looking for work."

"My child, now you bear a grudge against me for something I said to try and help you."

"No madam, I don't hold a grudge against you. I am very grateful, but it would be an abuse of your generosity if I remained."

"What are you saying? You are the lady of the house..."

"Thank you, but if you want my eternal gratitude, find, or help me find work."

"I will do all that is within me to make you happy but now go to bed and don't be so nervous. Good heavens, you look frightened, as if you had seen the devil. Go, go, good night my child."

"Good night, Madam," and with that she took her son by the arm and started going towards her room.

"What's this? What news is this?" Margherita yelled, "Aren't you going to give me the usual good night kiss?"

"You're right, I was distracted." Vittoria kissed the old lady on the forehead with trembling lips, impotent to hide the disgust she felt in kissing that woman now that she was aware of her malicious plans.

When the poor wretched girl was alone in her room, she burst out crying.

IX Conspiracy

As soon as Vittoria was in her room, Margherita approached her husband and shook him brutally. The drunkard woke up swearing but did not have time to show his bad mood, because Margherita quickly began speaking to him in a whisper telling what had just transpired with Vittoria.

"My dear," grumbled Napoleon, "I told you nothing would come of this. That woman has a look that reflects honesty a mile away."

"Fine," the woman replied, "we won't get anything with kindness, but we have other ways."

"Yes, but dangerous ways that can lead us directly to Sing Sing."

"You've been singing the same song for many years now, and if I had listened to you today, we would be dying of hunger.

"That devil of Ruizzi. I painted such a seductive portrait of the girl that wants to see her at any cost. He seems so restless, and he told me he will come tomorrow evening."

"Let him come, Vittoria will be his."

"Wife, loo ."

"Coward!"

"Do as you wish, but I pray you let's go to bed."

They lowered the folding bed, and, in that filthy kitchen, the worthy couple soon took their place, continuing their conversation, whispering under the sheets so as not to be understood by any living soul. Husband and wife, before closing their eyes, had plotted the ruin of the young mother, who at that same moment was crying and praying.

X THE NARCOTIC

Vittoria had not closed an eye all night, at the slightest noise she would jump up from her bed, startled and frightened, her heart pounding in such a way that is seemed it would break. At daybreak, tired and defeated, she fell asleep, but not a real sleep, more like a lethargy populated by wicked forms and frightful scenes. Her lethargy lasted until Margherita came to knock on her door to tell her it was time to get up. The old lady, wanting to deceive her victim, told her that in a couple of days she would find her work in a candy factory that belonged to one of the most respectable Italian families.

Vittoria would have preferred to leave the Mulberry Street house immediately, but since she had no place to go, she felt that she had to stay put. That day, Margherita did not leave her side for one minute and was kinder than usual. Napoleon did not show his face all day, not even for lunch at noon. A sure sign that his purse was full.

Napoleon returned home around six in the evening, and strangely he wasn't at all drunk. Dinner that evening was most refined and plentiful. Napoleon had even brought home a bottle of Rhine wine, made in California that when poured gave the glasses giving an amber color. When the couple lifted their glasses to drink that precious liquor, instead of bringing it to their lips they masterfully threw it over their shoulders. Vittoria did not eat much but drank a couple of glasses of that Rhine wine with great pleasure. Supper had just ended when the young lady felt a great weight on her head, her eyes began to close, and a general drowsiness began taking possession of her body. She wanted to struggle against the drowsiness, but she was helpless. Her son Enrico had also fallen into a deep sleep. When Vittoria stopped moving, Margherita ordered her husband to pick her up in his arms and take her to her room.

Napoleon didn't have to be told twice. He picked up the sleeping beauty like a feather, hugged her to his chest with a thrill of pleasure and set out for the room. His eyes twinkled like that of a cat, the contact with that perfect body was making his blood go to his brain, and if his wife hadn't been there, poor Vittoria would certainly have been raped by that brute. When Napoleon had set the woman on the bed his wife made him leave the room, and began to quickly undress Vittoria, who was sleeping ever more soundly. From the ceiling fixture a weak light illuminated the splendid form of the unfortunate creature who was about to become the victim of the most heinous attack.

XI Sold

When Margherita came out of Vittoria's room, her face was radiant.

"And so?" her husband asked her.

"All is going well. The girl is sleeping like a log, even cannon fire couldn't wake her."

"Ruizzi, when is he coming?"

"He'll be here in a bit. What are we going to do with the brat?"

"Put him in the small room and cover him with this quilt. He'll be fine."

Napoleon obeyed immediately. After about a half hour, hurried steps could be heard coming up the stairs and a few moments later a cautious knock on the door. Margherita hurried to open and Ruizzi, well dressed, elegant and perfumed, entered.

"Welcome, my lord," the woman said, "You are fortunate. I have prepared for you a beauty of the first order, as well as a woman of the highest virtue."

"I know you, Mamma Margherita, and I'm sure that you will treat me like a first-class client. Now, can I see the game."

"Certainly, look through that door."

The scene that unfolded in front of Ruizzi's eyes made his blood boil with lust; on the bed, with only a nightshirt to cover her, without hiding her sculpturesque profile, Vittoria was lying on the bed. Her voluminous black hair covered part of her face, making it impossible to see it from the shadows. The ceiling light concentrated its rays on the woman's bosom and showed it in all its opulence and candor.

Ruizzi was ready to throw himself on that beautiful body, when he felt himself restrained by Margherita's hand as she closed the door to the room.

"First, let's reason."

"Well, how much do you want?"

"The dangers are many, we are always on the road to Sing Sing, we need to think about what could go wrong..."

"Enough talk." How much?

"O.K. then, it seems that one hundred dollars..."

"Very well..."

"Then you have lodging expenses."

"What do they total?"

"Let's say one-hundred and fifty dollars."

Ruiz took from his pocket an elegant booklet covered in red leather, he opened his fountain pen and wrote on a 'Check' the sum of 150 dollars, and gave it to Margherita, who immediately made it disappear in her bosom.

"And now," Ruizzi said, "Leave. Leave the house to me."

"Certainly, we're leaving," answered Margherita, "but first I must tell you that the woman is asleep."

"My kisses will wake her."

"I don't think so, she took a narcotic."

"I would have preferred her awake."

"The she wouldn't be yours. Good luck."

XII Husband and Wife

As soon as Mr. and Mrs. Gherardini retired to their room, Ruizzi flung himself into Vittoria's room. With unbridled lust, his trembling hands touched her firm and wonderfully perfumed flesh, and, for a long time, pressed his lips to those of the beauty sleeping before his eyes. The bed's canopy blocked the lamp's feeble light and formed a shadow over Vittoria's face. Ruizzi, gasping for breath, with temples pounding, was overcome by a feeling of ecstasy that he was not used to. But he would have preferred that that body would reawaken and respond with equal passion to his caresses.

Suddenly it seemed to him that Vittoria moved. He waited anxiously, hugging the young woman tightly to his bosom. A few minutes passed when a sigh came from Vittoria's lips, and then her eyes opened. Immediately she didn't understand what was happening, but as she saw herself half naked in the arms of a man she let out a horrible yell, and freeing herself with a violent movement from those arms that held her like the coils of a serpent, she jumped from the bed, asking for help.

Quickly, Ruizzi was on top of her again. A savage fight ensued with Vittoria defending herself by biting and scratching the wicked individual that wanted to possess her. Ruizzi, inflamed and excited by her resistance, did not give ground. In the struggle, Vittoria's shirt was torn, and she found herself nude in the arms of the vile libertine. The poor soul was exhausted and the moment when she would have to cede was fastly approaching. Ruizzi's triumph was almost certain as he began to lower his victim on the bed and as he prepared to vent his bestial needs, Vittoria stopped defending herself....

Suddenly, a ray of light fell on the woman's face. Ruizzi recoiled, scared, and from his lips came the following:

"My wife!"

"Renato!" Vittoria replied.

There was a moment of silence. Then the man broke the silence, with a voice that was full of anger:

"What are you doing in America?"

"You're asking me? Your son and I have been looking for you"

"What are your intentions?"

"To live by your side, not for me, this was the last straw, and my heart will not yearn anymore for the wretch that entered this room to commit the most heinous of crimes, but for our son who has the right to a family."

"You will return immediately to Naples."

"Never."

"It's necessary." Ruizzi yelled with a threatening voice.

"I will remain by your side." She answered, not at all intimidated.

"That can't be and will not be, you will return."

"No."

"Do not challenge me. Listen, if you wish that someday I may return to Europe a rich and esteemed man, you must leave me."

"Never, never, I found you and I will stay. Not to love you, that's true but at least our son will have a father."

"Vittoria, I implore you, leave"

"It's no use, I will not leave."

"Vittoria, be careful!"

"What?"

"Desperation leads to crime."

"It would not be the first."

"What are you saying? Bitch."

"Do you remember why you left Naples..."

Ruizzi became livid, this woman wanted to ruin him as he was ready to assure his future with his forthcoming marriage into a rich family. Her appearance on the scene was about to bring his carefully constructed plan to a screeching halt. It could not be, it would not be.

To escape the danger that was threatening him, his wife had to return to Italy. He changed tactics and tried to convince her with kindness, but to no avail. Vittoria was adamant about not leaving.

Her opposition irritated Ruizzi. He treated his wife brutally, while she, resigned but firm, did not utter a lament.

But when Ruizzi, foaming at the mouth, yelled at her that it took some courage to bring to America a son that was not his, the martyr raised her head proudly, and exclaimed with conviction:

"You're a vile, miserable human being, fouler and more disgraceful than I thought could ever be possible."

Those insults hit Ruizzi like lashes to his face. He lost the light of reason and threw himself on his wife, his fingers in a death grip around her white neck.

Vittoria still had the strength to cry "Coward! Murderer!" then the words choked in her throat as Ruizzi maintained and tightened his grip. Her still body folded unto itself and dropped to the floor when the hands of her assailant stopped chocking and let her go.

It was then that Ruizzi realized what he had done. He had committed a new crime and was overwhelmed by a great fear. His future flashed before his eyes: the inquest, the trial, the conviction, the electric chair, and again he was overwhelmed by a great and indescribable fear; he quickly regained his cool headedness and thought of saving himself and not leave any traces of his passage. Furthermore, he was certain that the Gherardini would not betray him because they would also suffer the consequences. Ruizzi dressed himself and left the room where his wife's body was laying on the bed without as much as a single glance at the woman who had loved him so. While he was hurriedly going down the stairs, a young man, a little uncertain of himself, was slowly walking up. Ruizzi went right by him without paying any attention. When the assassin set foot on Mulberrry it was one in the morning.

XIII THE ARREST

The man Ruizzi almost ran into while he was running down the stairs after having committed the most horrible crime was Righetti, the young man passionately in love with Margherita. We will briefly describe why and how he was on the Gherardini's stairwell at that late hour of the night.

One can say that the young lover, forgetful of everything and attracted by an arcane, mysterious force to the house where the one who had taken possession of his heart lived, spent his life on Mulberry. Moreover, in that Italian neighborhood, much slandered and at the same time so picturesque, he found a piece of his faraway country, and the happiness that surrounded him rendered the first days of his exile less painful.

Righetti, preferred to stay across the street from the house where the joy of his heart was brought, hoping to see her as she went out. Asking questions here and there he became convinced that Vittoria was in great danger. Those countrymen, the majority from the Southern provinces, made him understand, with their brusque candor, that the Ghirendini had a horrible reputation and that all honest people should avoid them like the plague. The young man, who came to America with a small sum of money needed to confront the first necessities, had in his wallet about 1,000 francs, not a large sum in America but he was determined to use those meager resources to help the woman he loved.

Across the street from the Ghirendini house there was a large beer hall, not elegant, patronized by many Italians because the owner was very popular. Righetti made the beer hall in general quarters and basically stayed there from morning till night. The regulars, seeing this new face that no one knew, tried their best to figure out from what part of Italy he came from. The young man, who had no interest in lying, told them who he was and why he came to America.

The Italians, used to the hardest type of work, sympathized with all their hearts because they knew that America is a place suited only for men who had strong arms and backs to work, and understood that the young man, elegantly dressed, with a refined bearing and long white delicate hands, would soon run into the most painful disappointments.

When Ruizzi tried to take possession of the beautiful immigrant Margherita had sold him, Righetti was at his usual place in the beer hall. That evening the owner had kept the bar open longer than usual because of the serious discussion among the small colony of Italians; One of those discussions that always ended in nefarious battles and murders, where the Italian name would be brutalized and covered in mud. The owner of the beer hall, an influential man and leader of various associations, surrounded by many friends, was discussing the events of the day, and, in the heat of the discussion, did not realize that it was past midnight, the time that all beer halls should close. The policeman on the beat took it upon himself to remind the owner of his duties, and the owner quickly, but courteously, showed his clients the door.

Righetti was one of the last to leave. The weather was not good, it was gloomier than usual. The young man took a long look at the house where the idol of his heart lived and was ready to leave when he thought he heard a stifled cry that came from the Ghirendini's house. He listened carefully but did not hear anything. He dismissed it as a trick his mind was playing on him and began to leave but an internal voice kept on saying "it's a mistake to leave, Vittoria needs you."

"Well, I'll take a look." He whispered to himself. He crossed the street, entered the narrow alley, and, like a common thief, he staggered up the stairs that lead to the Gherandini's apartment. When he heard someone coming down the stairs, he was almost overcome by fear almost turned around, but love gave him courage and he continued up the stairs.

When Righetti reached the landing of the Gherardini's home he felt a pang in his heart when he saw the door wide open. Nonetheless, he entered determined to see why. There was no one in the kitchen. He crossed it with a steady step and moved towards the open door to Vittoria's room. As soon as he crossed the threshold, he let out a horrible, anguished cry and almost fainted.

The spectacle in front of his eyes was dreadful. The bed was unmade, the furniture strewn about, the curtains ripped, and in the middle of that confusion, like an ancient statue that's been toppled over, was the nude body of Vittoria. Righetti had an intuition of what must have happened, and cursed his destiny that made him arrive too late. On his knees on the rug, the young man looked for the slightest movement, hoping that the body in front of him was still alive. In the meantime, his desperate cry sounded the alarm, and the neighbors began to open windows and ask each other what could have happened; some said they heard cries, laments, and moans throughout the evening, while others suggested that it would be wise to call the police. That suggestion met with a consensus, and a young man took it upon himself to complete the mission.

Righetti, in tears, was uselessly trying to give life and warmth to that motionless body that seemed to have already received the cold kiss of death. When the policeman entered the room, Righetti was holding Vittoria's body tight to his bosom, and, overcome by his passion, was furiously kissing the beautiful woman that rested in his arms. He was awakened from his ecstasy by the policeman's rough voice, who yelled at him: "You are my prisoner."

Righetti did not understand the words, but feeling the policeman's hand on his shoulder he understood that he was being arrested. He had entered a house that wasn't his, so the policeman had every right to arrest him. Various neighbors, who entered the apartment behind the officer, saw the naked body of Vittoria and quickly ran to cover her, while giving Righetti, who could not comprehend why everyone was looking at him so menacingly, a look of contempt.

"Follow me," the policeman said abruptly, and to a detective, "John, you stay here until the ambulance arrives."

Righetti did not understand the words of the policeman and remained frozen in front of Vittoria's body, which the women had laid on the bed. The policemen brutally grabbed him by the shoulders and shoved him towards the door, the unlucky young man wanted to protest but the policeman raised his club and hit him repeatedly.

In the meantime, like a bolt of lightning, the news spread on Mulberry that a crime had been committed. The windows on both sides of the street opened noisily, and everyone was asking questions, asking for details of what happened. Like all news, even this was exaggerated: from one end to the other of the long street, the news was that an Italian had committed a horrendous crime and that he had killed at least four poor souls. The farther one went from the scene of the crime the event assumed larger and larger proportions. So that, when Righetti, who everyone already assumed was the murderer, appeared from the building in the hands of the police, a loud threatening cry went up from the crowd in the street, and repeated by the women at their windows in their nightshirts, oblivious to the cold. The rumbling, always louder, always more insulting and threatening, accompanied the poor man to police headquarters at the end of Mulberry, where, despite his protests, he was locked in a small narrow cell, with an iron gate and a filthy table.

To Righetti it all seemed like a bad nightmare. When the iron gate closed behind him, he asked himself more than once if he was sleeping or awake. Unfortunately for him, he wasn't dreaming, what was happening to him was a sad and tragic reality, and soon he would realize that he was being overcome by terrible events.

XIV. THE ACCUSATION

The hours that Righetti passed in the filthy police cell, were, for the poor soul an indescribable agony.

Certain that he did not commit any crime Righetti was not worried. He was sure that, after explaining what had happened, he would be cleared and set free. What anguished him was Vittoria's death, the woman he loved and to whom he had sworn all his affection.

In his heart a sense of vengeance was taking hold towards the individual who had abused and murdered Vittoria. He had no doubts that a crime was committed and that the author of the crime was the man he ran into while going up the stairs to Margherita's house.

"I'll find the coward," he kept on murmuring to himself, as he paced up and down like a caged animal, "I will find him, and then heaven help him!"

Then he would be overcome with doubts. Find him! How? Without friends, without contacts, with few means, in a large city he did not know, in the middle of an immense population, where even the best policemen lost traces of criminals.

The lover's meditations were interrupted by the yelling and cussing of the other prisoners the police where continuously bringing to the station. These were the drunks gathered along the way, full of bruises from their falls, or men with black and blue eyes from a beating they had received. Along with these filthy men came women who were even filthier, with their vests and dresses ripped to shreds, muddied from the dirty water on the street. The policemen brutally shoved those poor souls into those miserable cells and answered their cries and groans with their nightsticks, contempt, laughter and a string of obscenities. This was the nightly show that took place among the steel gates, the heavy doors, under the eyes of the guards, who, used to the recurring spectacle, sat with their legs propped up, reading the first news of the day. Finally dawn arrived, the light from the gas lamps paled and the hallways were suddenly full of people, the janitors began sweeping the pavement, cleaning the gates and polishing the locks.

Around eight a bell sounded, and, soon after, the cells were unlocked, and the servants began the distribution of coffee, milk and bread. It was time for breakfast, welcomed by the joyous sounds of the detained. Righetti wanted nothing to do with his ration. He was anxiously waiting to be interrogated and then set free.

At ten the arresting office came for him. He was very happy but when they tried to put the cuffs on him, he backed off.

The policeman, without niceties, grabbed Righetti's arms, who shivered from indignity and shame when he felt the cold steel that circled his wrists, as if they were those of a common criminal.

The prisoner was brought on foot to the Tombs. All along the way people stopped to stare at him and a group of curiosity seekers followed. The wretch, confused and red from shame, felt he was going to die under the sarcastic looks that followed him without pity. Finally, they arrived at the Tombs, a depressing granite building, a frightful edifice that injects a sinister note in one of the busiest streets of New York. Righetti went up the stairs as the crowd moved to the sides, all the while looking at him threateningly.

The hall of the tribunal of the Tombs was also full of people. The morning newspapers had published in great detail the crime that happened on Mulberry. The reporters had also made things up about Righetti and painted him as one of those ferocious animals, horrible in affairs of love, cruel in their vengeance, and bloodthirsty. Furthermore, they added that since he was an Italian accused of being wicked and dangerous, to lynch him would be an act of grace.

Since Judge Trainit did not begin to administer justice until eleven, Righetti had to wait in a holding cell a good half hour before being called to his hearing. That time was well spent by the reporters who took photos of the assassin.

Finally, it was time to go in front of the judge. The poor wretch thought that he would be allowed to explain why he entered the house of persons he did not know, and that since he did it with good intentions he hoped to be pardoned and set free.

When Righetti found himself in front of the judge, the arresting officer went into a long narration. They were words that made no sense to the prisoner. When the policeman finished, the judge said: "Good. Take the accused and bring him to 'City Prison' and kept in custody until further clarification." The policeman was handed a file from the Judge and said to the prisoner: "Let's go!"

What! They were taking him away without letting him speak, without saying a word? Was he free? He interrogated the officer. It was useless, he didn't know Italian. The interpreter approached him and said:

"You can't be judged here for your crime; you have to see other judges."

"My crime! What am I accused of? Speak to me. In the name of God tell me."

"You don't know? You are accused of attempted murder, for vengeance, of a young lady recently arrived from Italy."

"Me, a murderer!" He yelled in a voice choked by emotion. He didn't say more, the news hit him too hard, and the poor soul lost his senses and fell backwards as though he were dead.

The people in the hall started whispering, and everyone wanted to see what had happened. The policemen on duty had a hard time controlling the crowd, while two of them took the prisoner and led him back to the cells by the stairwell that connected the Tribunal with the Tombs.

When Righetti woke up three hours later he occupied cell number 69 in the Tombs, one of the drearier in the dreariest of buildings.

XV INSANE!

The officer who arrested Righetti had called for an ambulance from Chambers Street Hospital. The ambulance arrived quickly and transported Vittoria to the hospital. Since this was classified a crime, the doctors on call made a careful exam of the body which had all the rigidity and appearance of a cadaver. The results of their preliminary diagnosis made them aware that the woman was alive but that her condition was serious.

Vittoria remained between life and death for eight days, if you could call living that deep coma that the doctors could not explain. The doctors surmised that it was a miracle that poor woman had not been strangled; the nails of the assassin had penetrated the skin around her neck, leaving wounds and bruises all around her neck.

During the ninth day of her hospital stay, Vittoria began to recover her senses, her arms and legs started losing their stiffness and her blood began to circulate. Only her eyes remained shut.

When, after so many days, the poor soul reopened her eyes she began to furiously toss and turn, and agonizing shrieks came from her lips that were streaked with white foam. At times she was plagued by terror and wanted to flee from her bed, at other times she begged for pity. She was often threatening, her voice became hard and bitter, and her stare hard and frightful. The doctors did not hesitate to give their diagnosis, Vittoria Ruiz was insane.

When Righetti came to, it took him a while to gather his thoughts, but he finally began remembering. Passionate tears flowed down his cheeks to think that he was suspected of killing the woman he loved! How? Why? Was justice so blind to commit such errors. Suddenly, he let out a cry of joy. He remembered that the interpreter told him that he was accused of attempted suicide, attempted. That meant that there was no murder. Vittoria was alive!

She lived! What a feeling of immense relief he felt. What did he care about being in that cell, Vittoria's deposition would open the prison doors for him, and maybe the event could also serve to bring him the greatest happiness. Righetti, fully reassured, threw himself on the steel cot with the hard straw mattress that occupied more than half of the cell, and slept soundly. He was awakened in the evening by the servers that brought him bread and soup. He was hungry and avidly ate his bread and soup, if you could actually call that mixture soup. That night, Righetti rested peacefully, and dreamt a thousand beautiful things, as though he were sleeping in a palace instead of a squalid cell in the Tombs.

The days passed and it seemed that everyone forgot about the prisoner. During the two hours of daily exercise, which consisted of walking up and down the narrow terraces that circle the cells of the three floors of the Tombs, Righetti had a chance to speak to other Italians, also awaiting their trial. They advised him to turn to an Italian lawyer, and gave him the address of a young lawyer, talented and with good intentions, to who Righetti immediately wrote a long letter.

The lawyer accepted Righetti's invitation. He listened attentively to what Righetti had to say and came away convinced that the young man was innocent of the crime he was accused of committing.

"Besides," Righetti concluded, "Vittoria is alive, and she will tell them who rally tried to abuse her and kill her."

"Don't deceive yourself, my friend," the lawyer answered, "Vittoria will not vindicate you."

"What, do you also believe that she is guilty?"

"No, no: but there are other insurmountable motives. You see, the young woman you love, is..."

"Well..."

"I wouldn't want to..."

"Tell me, tell me. Now I have to know everything."

"Maybe it is better that you know. Vittoria is insane."

"Insane! Insane!" he cried as he burst into tears.

"Do not despair, we'll get you off nonetheless."

"What do I care. I would rather be in a chain gang than know that the woman I love suffers so."

The lawyer did not know how to answer and to hide his emotions he left.

Two weeks later the Grand Jury indicted Alfredo Righetti for attempted murder in the first degree.

Vittoria, whose madness worsened, was brought to Blackwell's Island.

The small Enrico, who invoked his mother with pitiful cries, was turned over to the Gerry Association.

The Ghirendini's were never seen again on Mulberry. This made an impression on the whole neighborhood, and Inspector Byrne, who has a nose for these things, took note of this and promised himself to get to the bottom of the mystery of that disappearance.

Renato Ruiz spent those first days after the crime in anguish. When he learned from the papers that Vittoria was not dead, he thought of fleeing, but too many business interests tied him to New York that he stayed despite the danger he faced. When he read that his wife was declared insane and incurable, he felt a delirious joy. He was safe and he could complete his plans without impunity.

For the man that was in jail for his crime, not even a thought, besides, he had his trial and was found not guilty. Justice was served and the case was closed.

Vittoria's voice could not be heard from the depths of the asylum. Everything was going as well as could be. Renato was triumphant.

Part IV

Friends

Salvatore Bancheri

Paolo Giordano
A Life of Friendship and Dedication

In January 2024, Paolo Giordano sent me a brief email expressing his desire to contribute an article to the *Festschrift* in honor of our mutual friend, Michael Lettieri. His message filled me with joy but also surprised me, as I knew he was going through a particularly difficult time due to his health. Despite the challenges, he met every deadline with remarkable dedication—more promptly than many other contributors.

I begin with this episode to highlight Paolo's deep humanity and the value he has always placed on friendship. Over the years, a strong bond developed between the American triad of Giordano-Pietralunga-Tamburri and the Canadian triad of Bancheri-Colilli-Lettieri, reflected in our contributions to Festschrifts for both Lettieri and Paul Colilli.

Our friendship, both personal and professional, grew through many AATI conferences. It likely began at my first AATI meeting in New York in 1986 and deepened over time. Paolo played a central role in the Association, holding every executive position—from Secretary-Treasurer to President—and (co-)organizing major conferences, including those in Genoa (2006) and Taormina (2008). His immense contributions were recognized in 2009 with the *AATI Distinguished Service Award*, honoring his impact as a scholar, teacher, and leader in Italian Studies.

To me, Paolo has been more than a friend — he played a key role in my professional growth. It was thanks to him that I became involved in AATI leadership, particularly during his presidency (2006-2007), when he entrusted me with updating the Association's webpage, creating the listserv, and, most importantly, developing the membership database. He also appointed me as Director of Communication, a role I held from 2007 to 2013. His foresight led to my later roles as Secretary-Treasurer (2010-2013), President (2015-2017), and Past President (2018-2019).

Among my fondest memories with Paolo, two stand out. One is a dinner during the AATI conference in Genoa, where, alongside colleagues and friends, we spent an unforgettable evening sharing stories, reminiscing, and laughing as we tried to outdo each other with jokes. The other is the Taormina conference, where, in addition to handling registration matters, we spent long hours talking about ourselves, our families, and our friends — conversations that now hold even greater meaning.

But the most touching moment was Paolo's presence at the AATI conference in Chicago in November 2023. Given his fragile health, none of us expected him to attend. Yet, he insisted on joining us to celebrate AATI's centennial alongside past presidents and longtime colleagues. His speech moved us all — a testament to his immense humanity and deep dedication to his profession.

Anthony, Paolo, Michael • AATI 100 Years, 2023

More than ever on that occasion, I felt honored to be counted among his friends. Thank you, Paolo, for your guidance, your inspiration, and above all, your friendship.

TVB. 💗💗💗💗💗

Salvatore Bancheri, University of Toronto

TED CACHEY

Paolo was not impressed, nor was he very enthusiastic about working with me when we first met 40 years ago. I know because he told me, right off the bat.

One of my first assignments as a starting visiting assistant professor at Arizona State University was to accompany the students on the joint ASU-Rosary College Florence summer program with Paolo. The late Piero Baldini, who had founded the program together with Paolo, could not join the trip. I was drafted to fill in, fresh from grad school.

I can't remember his exact words, but Paolo let me know he wasn't crazy about having such a greenhorn as his partner. Luckily, Anna Maria and Rosa hit it off. I started learning the ropes from Paolo right away and survived the summer.

Working with Paolo on study abroad that summer turned into of one of the most memorable, instructive, and fun friendships I've been fortunate to have had in the profession. Wonderful memories I can't go into here. And the list of things I learned from Paolo, by watching him "operate" professionally, is long. (I don't think Paolo would be offended by the term.) He was always looking out for opportunities to make a contribution, regularly taking on new challenges in teaching, research, and higher education leadership. An observer from the sidelines, I have followed with immense admiration the creation of Italian American studies by Paolo, together with Anthony and Fred over the last 40 years. Having worked with Paolo I can imagine how much fun the "Bordighera boys" have all had together accomplishing this feat.

So it goes without saying how pleased I am to be able to join other colleagues who have been fortunate enough to work with Paolo, in sending him happy birthday wishes, and greetings to Rosa too, from Anna Maria and me.

Ted Cachey
University of Notre Dame

Ryan Calabretta-Sajder

Paolo Giordano: Teacher, Scholar, Mentor

Paolo Giordano has always been "phantasmic" for me.

As an undergraduate at Dominican University, his name was ever-present throughout Lewis and Mazzuchelli Halls. I remember stopping in Lewis Hall one afternoon and speaking with Sister Philip Mary Reilly about Professor Giordano's interview when he first came to campus and the impression he made with the Dominican Sisters. In another conversation with Sister Melissa Waters, I was told about Professor Giordano's legacy with the students, particularly the Italian American DU community. A particular story was shared about Giordano consoling not only a student but also the family during the mourning of a recently passed loved one. I recall reading Giordano's Italian Renaissance scholarship with Rosalind Hays in an independent study course on "Why the Renaissance? Why Florence?" in order to finish my Certificate and Medieval Studies. Other faculty like Chris Como recalled playing racquetball with Giordano while on faculty.

When I studied abroad in Florence, Italy through the consortium with DU, Arizona State U, Purdue U, etc., Giordano was regularly mentioned as the founder of our relationship with the program, a great professor, and an amazing mentor. Giordano was also a household name for the parents of all my friends at Dominican, as all of them studied with him. During his time at Dominican and later at Loyola University, Chicago, he trained a generation of K-12 and university professors. He worked closely with them and pushed many to pursue graduate studies, even when their parents discouraged them. Giordano left a lasting impression on Dominican University.

When I joined the Executive Council of AATI, again, I heard again about the legacy of Giordano in his many roles in the organization. First, he served as Secretary/Treasurer from 1988-1990, later as Secretary from 1996-2000, Vice-President from 2004-2005, and then President from 2006-2007. Under Albert Mancini's Editorship of *Italica*, Giordano served as Associate Editor for almost a decade. Giordano's extensive service to the AATI lead to his 2009 Distinguished Service Award from the Association. Over the years, he has organized numerous conferences, helped publish over 40 issues of *Italica*, and promoted the Association locally, nationally, and internationally.

The first scholarly publication of Giordano's that I recall engaging with is *From the Margin: Writings in Italian Americana* (1991). Known as the one of the first "Bibles" of Italian American studies, this anthology and its sequel, *Beyond the Margin: Readings in Italian Americana* (1998) assisted in solidifying the field for years to come.

Although I have known Paolo Giordano for many years through conferences and AATI activities, I never truly knew him until studying Joseph Tusiani. As many know, Tusiani, the first recipient of the AATI Distinguished Service Award and the Poet Laureate Emeritus of New York, published widely througout his career. Giordano's research on the Poet Laureate is some of the most extensive and rich scholarship from North America. Giordano's exploration of Tusiani's lyric through his work with *Gente mia* and novel/memoir with "The Writer Suspended between Two Worlds: Joseph Tusiani's 'Autobiografia di un italo-americano'" illustrates

Tusiani's significance and charts a clear evolution of the Italian American author. Giordano's work on Tusiani has inspired me to more deeply investigate his opus, rereading some previously studied poetry, but also considering understudied works.

Paolo Giordano has always been "phantasmic" for me. I have learned about his legacy through the halls of Dominican University, the conferences of AATI, the classes of *La scuola italiana* of Middlebury College, the multitude of articles in *Italica*, his academic scholarship celebrating the migrant authors, the generation of excellent Italian teachers in Chicago and bound, and the plethora of stories from others documented in this volume, especially Fred Gardaphè and Anthony Julian Tamburri.

As "phantasmic" as Paolo has seemed over the years, with others singing his praise and sharing his accolades, he has always been present. He has been a cherished friend, mentor, and collaborator. He warmly invited me to join a session on Tusiani at an AATI@ACTFL conference, which later produced a "special section" in *Italica* 93.2 (Summer 2016). He has also given advice on the tenure process and career mentorship at large. Paolo is a true teacher/scholar.

ANNA CAMAITI HOSTERT

I first met Paolo when he came to Loyola University of Chicago many years ago. I had moved from Italy recently and I was teaching there. I found in him a person to whom I could speak in Italian about Italy without having to explain everything about it. I even called him Paolo instead of Paul as everyone else used to do in the States.

We shared feelings, experiences and differences. As an academic administrator, he was very fair and always promoted and helped teachers.

Paolo is a generous person who has a sharp sense of humor and a strong sense of family. We became friends and I remember several times to have been at his and Rosa's parties and have met his mother toward whom he was very affectionate. I also remember the dedication to his wife, his daughters Michèle, Stephanie and their families.

When Paolo and I first met I was already acquainted with Anthony Tamburri who in those days was a professor at Purdue University. Paolo and Anthony share a friendship/brotherhood since they were kids in Connecticut. And in fact, they started together the publishing house by the name Bordighera Press from the name of the town in Liguria where Paolo was born and from which he maintained the accent when he spoke Italian. That publishing house has been a reference point for many of us who at the beginning of our career in the United States wanted to publish subjects and themes new or different from the mainstream.

In addition, Paolo, with Anthony Tamburri and Fred Gardaphe, established something new for the academic world in United States: the field of Italian/American Studies which took decades to become popular and acclaimed. Now even Italian universities teach that subject, thanks to them.

Paolo worked tirelessly toward that goal, especially because of his own experience as someone born in Italy, grown up and educated in the States. He always understood the uneasiness of a person who lives between two cultures and, also, contributed a great deal to the field of Italian/American Literature. He has edited several publications among which I want to remember the one regarding the selected poems of Joseph Tusiani. You could talk to him about many subjects, but you could tell that the field of Italian/American studies really made him passionate.

Paolo is a man of action and very capable of organizing events as in the case of the Italian language. Who can forget the very many initiatives from the one at the Middlebury College to the one at the Chicago Italian Institute of Culture to promote the Italian language, or his prominent roles in the many organizations of teachers of Italian?

In summary, Paolo is a man who was instrumental in the innovation of academic matters who also helped to promote the Italian language and culture.

Anna Camaiti Hostert
Università Tor Vergata, Rome

Peter Carravetta

Thoughts about My Friend Paolo

I don't exactly remember the first time I met Paolo, but it certainly goes back to the early 90s, when I was introduced to him through his old friend Anthony Tamburri, I believe at Purdue, during one of their Annual Conferences in Romance Languages and Cinema, a year or two before he co-edited and published *From the Margin*. Those years were intense. It seemed that at every professional gathering, we would end up discussing — often with a cohort of *compagni di cordata* — questions about our identity, from where and when we came to the U.S., how the local communities viewed and received us, how complicated assimilation was, and yet interested in introducing new voices and critical paradigms. Paolo was director of the Loyola University Rome Center when I was a Fulbright Fellow there in 1991, and he, knowing Rome, was so helpful and supportive, and interested in my studies. Despite heavy institutional responsibilities, he managed to find time to study the Baroque and 16th century Genovese poetry.

In the states, he interviewed me for *The Canadian Journal of Italian Studies* in which he got me to express a complex web of relations which he understood, sympathized with, and then encouraged me to stick with the commitment to our fields, our professional objectives, a cultural politics which was coming out from under the radar. We set quite an agenda: struggle for a recognition of, and as, Italian writers in America (we'd discuss: were they expatriates, exiles, emigrants, [cultural] refugees, or even unemployed or wandering young professors? And what about those who were born there and then came here at an early age?) And the equally challenging campaign to explore, describe, put on the academic map Italian American studies, starting with its writers. In that context, Paolo has an impressive record of promoting, editing, and translating Italian and Italian American authors.

Paolo contributed so much to both fields, true to an intellectual ideal that spans centuries, countries, and generations. In this context, our discussions about what is an identity often brought us to consider whether perhaps we all have *volens nolens* several identities (without being schizophrenic!). Just a matter of recognizing them. And living them. We often enjoyed talking about the idiosyncrasies present in our backgrounds, the foibles of venturing across some unseen border (of class, language, economics, intellectual community), and how at times we had to resort to a hearty laughter to avoid being depressed at some absurd contingencies. Paolo always had a healthy sense of realism. And a sense of humor. As I said, *mi ha dato sempre grande gioia rivederlo*.

Paolo and his wonderful Rosa (and Michèle and Stephanie, of course) have been so pleasant every time I met with them, often over dinner, many times as a guest in their house, and if it weren't an over abused expression in Italian American circles, I would say he made you feel like you were "family." And that ain't such a bad thing, is it? *Il fratellone tra due mondi.*

Andrea Ciccarelli

My first sighting of Paul (but I confess that I have always called him Paolo) Giordano – or better of his name – was in the Chair's office in the department of French and Italian at Indiana University in 1990. I had just arrived to start as a newly appointed assistant professor and my eyes fell on the shelves that displayed the departmental dissertations. I read the various titles that, at the time, were mostly what we would expect for a department of languages and cultures, except that there was this 1978 dissertation on the Italian migration to Louisiana that stood out and caught my attention. I picked it up and began reading the preface on the origins, effects and results of this mostly unknown 19th-century Italian presence in Louisiana.

I thought that whoever this Giordano was, he certainly had intellectual courage and independence to study and write on a subject that seemed, at the time, *a latere* of what was then, the mainstream interests of Italian studies. Little I knew that, through the lively common denominator of the late Edoardo Lebano — my new colleague and Paul's dissertation advisor — we would meet soon, and it would be the beginning of a cordial, strong and stimulating professional and friendly relationship, as proven by the publication that we co-edited in 1998 (*L'esilio come certezza. La ricerca d'identità culturale in Italia dalla Rivoluzione francese ai nostri giorni*), a bilingual book that still receives many praises for its attempt to explore, as thoroughly as possible, the meaning of cultural identity in Italy and abroad, including the opportunity to identify and recognize the essence of what

Italian American can mean and embrace, besides the mere geo-cultural reference.

This is not the place to stress Paul's many contributions to Italian/ Italian American studies, to migration culture, to the profession in general, but one aspect of Paul that stands out, not differently than the title of his dissertation, is his ability to make people feel at ease in any environment, no matter if running into them at a conference, on the streets of Florence or in an airport. His talent to talk about professional and cultural matters, while also touching softer subjects, without ever sounding frivolous or distracted is a gift that can be imitated but not acquired. This is a trait of his character that, perhaps, can be explained best looking at the famous Bordighera paintings by Monet, especially Monet's Villa at Bordighera, which, through the delicate and yet firm color of the branches and trees, hide and reveal, precisely, what we need to see of the town and of the landscape.

José Fernandez

Paolo Giordano: A Man for all Peoples

In 2004, the University of Central Florida (UCF) was extremely fortunate to hire Dr. Paolo Giordano as Chair of the Department of Modern Languages and Literatures. A prolific scholar in the field of Italian and Italian-American literature, Paolo, also became the recipient of the Dr. Neil Euliano Endowed Chair in Italian Studies at UCF. In 2006, when I became Dean of the recently created College of Arts and Humanities, I had the opportunity to work closely with Paolo in advancing the mission and vision of our college.

As a teacher, Paolo, was a champion in language pedagogy. His three approaches to teaching Italian language and literature which combined the topical, the unstructured, and the personal gained him the respect and admiration of his colleagues and students.

As a researcher, Paolo's record consecrated him as one of the scholars par excellence in Italian-American literature. Paolo, along with Dr. Anthony Tamburri and others, helped to transform a field suffering from benign neglect, to one that is now part and parcel of the American literary panorama. At the same time, Paolo's works, helped Italian Americans in understanding their heritage from a collective humanistic perspective. Moreover, Paolo's unselfishness as a scholar, inspired others to follow the path he started.

As someone who spent 28 years of his 45-year academic career as an administrator, I rate Paolo as one of the top five administrators that I have ever encountered. Paolo was the consummate administrator who put people first and led by example. As departmental chair, he was tenacious and firm, yet, he was polished in manners, and being a people's person, he had the" right stuff" to deal with all kinds of individuals. An independent thinker, yet, a chain of command adherent, he always displayed a critical knowledge regarding the role of an administrator. Consequently, he commanded the attention and respect of superiors and subordinates. A skillful diplomat, excellent listener, and collegiate decision maker, Paolo was a top visionary who possessed the salient qualities of realizing his vision, not through intimidation, but rather through cooperation and mutual respect.

Not all my interactions with Paolo, revolved around budgets, faculty positions, goals and measures. Being both fierce football and soccer fans, we were always talking trash about my Minnesota Vikings and his Chicago Bears. Paolo also was an ardent Genoa fan and often berated me for being a rabid Juventus fan. I, however, liked to tease him by telling him, okay, Paolo, what you are saying about Juventus may be true, but how many *scudetti* has Genoa won?

This piece would not be complete without saying something about Rosa, Paolo's beloved wife. Throughout Paolo's career, Rosa has been Paolo's number one supporter. Her openness, charm, talent, and sense of humor put people at ease and bring out the best of them. Paolo and Rosa, Mimi and I remember that lovely lunch at Il Pirata on the Amalfi coast, and the cool nights at La Minerveta in Sorrento.

Paolo Giordano, character, integrity, gentle and kind, and a man for all peoples.

TERESA GIANNINI

Dear Professor Giordano,

it has been many years since I last saw you and your lovely wife. I had the pleasure of studying Italian at Rosary College and studying abroad in Florence, Italy in 1984 with you as our Professor. It was, by far, one of the best times of my life. Even after almost 41 years, I speak of that summer with such great fondness and beautiful memories. I met so many wonderful students, many of whom I am still friends with today. You were such an incredible teacher, guide, role model, leader and friend to us all. I remember you advising us to "be careful" with the Italian boys. A few of us, include-ing myself, fell in love with a charming Italian that summer. You looked out for us all as if we were your own children. I am forever grateful to you for instilling the love of Italy in us. The love and connection I have for Italy and for you will always remain in my heart. I hope our paths cross again soon. I would love to see you and your family again.

Wishing you all the best! Tante belle cose!

Sincerely, Teresa Giannini

Maria Iusco

Per Paolo

Carissimo Professor Giordano, Vorrei approfittare di questa possibilità per esprimere tutta la mia gratitudine per l'enorme influenza positiva che ha avuto sulla mia vita. Mi ricordo delle Sue lezioni come se fosse solo ieri e parlo del lontano 1985, 1986 e 1987. Erano un'occasione di crescita accademica ma anche una fonte di ispirazione per la mia vita personale. Grazie per avermi insegnato tanti valori importanti come la perseveranza, l'impegno, e l'importanza del pensiero critico. Le Sue lezioni mi hanno sempre accompagnato in tutti questi anni al punto di intraprendere anche io l'insegnamento della lingua italiana all'University di Illinois e di anche accompagnare centinaia di studenti in Italia ogni anno come Direttrice di Study Abroad. Incontrare persone che riescono a lasciare un'impronta così profonda è davvero una cosa rara ma Lei è una di queste persone e per questo La ringrazio. Grazie di cuore per tutti gli anni bellissimi a Rosary College e per questi ricordi indelebili. La penso sempre con tanto affetto e stima. Un augurio a Lei e alla Sua bellissima famiglia che ricordo molto bene.

Con rispetto,
Maria Iusco, Rosary College 1987

Michael Lettieri

It is an honor to write this tribute to you, carissimo Paolo—a cherished friend, colleague, teacher, scholar, educational administrator, publisher, associate editor of a premier scholarly journal, husband, father, and grandfather to Isabell, Sophie, and Beatrice. In whatever role I have known you, and from whatever vantage point, you have always stood out as someone very special.

We first met in the mid-eighties at one of the AATI annual conferences; then in 1988 we spent an entire summer together on the Middlebury College campus. Those first encounters (Giorni e ricordi che non scompaiono mai!) marked the beginning of our longstanding professional friendship and collaboration.

I have known you for over forty years and it is difficult not to use superlatives when talking about you. Really, how does one describe your amazing essence and spirit, your selfless generosity, your uncompromising belief in all that is good, and your unwavering commitment to work, family, and friends? Words cannot truly capture what you mean to so many people on so many levels.

You have excelled in many academic roles, including secretary treasurer and president of the AATI, chair of the Department of Modern Languages and Literatures at Loyola University (Chicago), director and academic dean of the Loyola University Rome Center for the Liberal Arts, associate editor of *Italica*, co-founder of Bordighera Press, and, last but not least, chair of the Department of Modern Languages and Literatures at the University of Central Florida.

You have been a truly exceptional teacher. You have produced some of the most important books in our field, both as an author and as a publisher. Your articles and oral presentations have found a large and receptive audience. You have proven your merit as an inspiring and creative administrator. You have been passionate about making our Italian classrooms better places for students to learn and for teachers to work. You have been a transformational leader and a change agent; a visionary who has shared and encouraged great dreams of what teaching and learning can be. Your gift for innovative thinking and your tenaciousness have been instrumental in successfully achieving meaningful educational progress. In terms of service to the profession, caro Paolo, you are a national treasure.

In addition to your devotion to your work and to the improvement of education locally and globally, you have always found time for your colleagues, your friends, and especially for Rosa, and Michèle and Stephanie and their families.

Through your actions, conduct, and values, you have been a role model for many of us. You have showed us what is possible. You have encouraged us to strive for excellence. And, oftentimes, you have challenged us. You have helped us to set and achieve ambitious goals.

Even as right now you are battling your illness, your commitment to your family, your work, your colleagues, and your friends never wavers. You continue to face each day with grace and determination, inspiring us all with your resilience and strength.

I have always appreciated your knowledge, humility, humanity, humor, optimism, professionalism, and conviction.

But what I am especially grateful for are the memories we share of our time together, in the Italian School at Middlebury College, at the numerous AATI conferences in North America and in Italy, during your trip to Canada and my visit to Loyola University many years ago.

It has been a privilege for me to have been a part of your life. Your friendship is a true treasure and a gift I cherish every day.

Fin quando, caro Paolo, il ricordo dei nostri giorni più lieti vivrà nei nostri cuori, dirò sempre che la vita è gioia e felicità!

Con grande affetto e profonda gratitudine,
Michele

Chiara Mazzucchelli

Il mio amico Paolo

It was the summer of 2002, and I had just been awarded a Fulbright fellowship to pursue my Ph.D. in the U.S. I was set to meet with the professor who had accepted me into the Ph.D. Program in Comparative Studies at Florida Atlantic University, Anthony Tamburri, at a conference at the Università di Messina. That day, Anthony introduced me to

his good friend and colleague, Paolo Giordano. At the time, I had no idea how significant that introduction would become in my professional and personal life.

Exactly five years later, in 2007, with my Ph.D. in hand, I met Paolo once again, this time in Orlando, where I had landed a one-year visiting position at University of Central Florida. It was early August; that kind of oppressive Florida heat that makes you question your life choices. And there was Paolo, in dress pants, a long-sleeve shirt, and a tie! He had a full beard then and was scratching it while explaining to me the expectations for the position. My first thought was, *mamma mia,* who's gonna save me from this department chair?

I couldn't have been more wrong.

As a chair, Paolo was fair but firm. He never shied away from tackling uncomfortable topics with faculty, often making department meetings an entertaining affair! From him, I learned one of the most valuable lessons of my career: to truly serve a university, one must understand its inner workings. "Learn the ropes of administration and how the sausage is made," he used to say, and I took that advice to heart. I will always be grateful for his mentorship.

As a professor, Paolo was beloved by his students. His lectures on the Renaissance left an indelible mark on those fortunate enough to sit in his classroom. His passion for teaching and deep knowledge of his field made him an unforgettable presence at UCF.

But to me, Paolo is more than a former chair and colleague, he is a dear friend. To this day, whenever something particularly amusing or downright absurd happens at UCF, in Florida or anywhere in the world, my first instinct is to call him from my car on the drive home.

Some colleagues drift apart over time, especially after one's retirement, but true friendships endure. Here's to many more phone calls, shared laughs over academic gossip, and reminders of why the best part of academia isn't just what we teach or read or write, but the people we meet along the way.

Chiara Mazzucchelli
University of Central Florida

Ambra Meda

I landed at MCO on a humid Sunday evening in the summer of 2011, weighed down with two big suitcases, a carry-on, a backpack, and a laptop bag. It was my first time leaving Europe, and I knew I wouldn't have been back for at least eleven months. I stood still under the glaring 'Arrivals' sign, like an islet of uncertainty in the bustling crowd. With no line on my Italian cell phone, I clung to the hope that my new department director would remember about the email I'd sent him the day before.

Shortly after, Paolo Giordano pulled up in his car, with his wife Rosa beside him, holding a bag with clean towels, soap and a box of homemade cookies. Their kindness wrapped around me like a warm blanket as they welcomed me to what was about to become my new home and accompanied me as I embarked on the most life-changing adventure I'd ever had.

From the day I met Paolo at a literature conference in Florence in the fall of 2010, it didn't take long to realize how much of a 'driving force' he really is. Before writing this piece, I went through the first emails we exchanged to bring those memories back to life. In just four months — and amidst Thanksgiving and Christmas — we managed to establish an international student exchange program between the University of Parma (where I used to teach) and the University of Central Florida, submit and get approved two panels for different literary conferences, curate a translation project from start to finish, and arrange my transfer to teach at UCF, navigating all the necessary approvals, paperwork and formalities that such an endeavor entails.

I watched him coordinate dozens of people, all with different roles, across two countries, move nimbly through the stumbling blocks of bureaucracy and rally others to his vision. "Paolo, ma sei davvero un vulcano!", I wrote to him in one of those early emails. As usual, he responded with one of his trademark 'two cents': "When you have an idea that seems valid, you must get things moving right away. If you overthink it, the moment passes, you get caught up in imaginary problems, and trouble almost always arises".

I learned that this is just who Paolo is when I started working at UCF, where he ran our department like a leader, never like a boss. Through his passion, enthusiasm, and the best kind of self-deprecating irony, he would encourage us to embrace his pragmatism, steering us away from what he called "the professorial habit of talking things to death". He inspired us to bring Italian literature and culture closer to students and general readers, advocating for translation efforts that could act as bridges between audiences and works on opposite sides of the ocean, and for a writing style that shunned academic technicalities in favor of reaching a broader crowd.

Beyond his professional persona, Paolo stands out to me as the one person who singlehandedly changed my life in the most profound way. Not only did he offer me the chance to move to the U.S., opening up a new chapter and a new path forward, but he also championed every one of my ambitions. Whether it was encouraging my scholarly pursuits or supporting my desire to explore the world beyond academia, Paolo cheered me on at every step. I am deeply grateful for his unwavering friendship, thoughtful hospitality and the countless lessons I keep learning from him — from how he faces challenges to the wisdom he drops without even trying.

Michelina Lieggi Mantovano

Stimato Professore Giordano,

Sono passati ben 46 anni dall'ultima volta in cui ci siamo visti in quell'aula ubicata dentro Lewis Hall presso Rosary College (oggi Dominican University). I ricordi sono tanti, e sono tutti serrati nel cuore. A tutt'oggi conservo, in una scatola ricordi, vari compiti ed esami da Lei corretti con vari commenti. Di tanto in tanto li leggo sorridendo con affetto.

Io Lo ricordo come un uomo affabile e caloroso. La Sua intelligenza era luminosa, e noi studenti eravamo nutriti da quella luce ed intelletto. La Sua grandezza vive con la conoscenza e le tante virtù che Lei ha trasmesso a generazioni e generazioni di studenti.

Per me, Professor Giordano, la memoria dei giorni in aula ascoltandoLa durante varie lezioni, che rimarranno scolpiti nel mio cuore.

La saluto calorosamente con un fortissimo ed affettuoso abbraccio,

Michelina Lieggi Mantovano

EMANUELE PETTENER & ILARIA SERRA

Carissimo Paolo,

Chiara (Mazzucchelli) and I have a running joke that we repeat every time we see each other: "I envy you for one reason," and she replies: "I know, I know: Paolo".

And it's so true. Working with you and under your guidance would have been truly beautiful, inspiring, fun. But — even if it wasn't possible, except for a couple of nice projects with Bordighera Press — I've always felt your friendship over the years to be vigorous, warm and comforting. A few years ago, Ilaria and I, with our children, escaped from a hurricane, and you and Rosa, also on the run, had the extraordinary kindness to invite us into the safe apartment you had rented. It was a wonderful week's vacation, Rosa's exquisite cooking, the conversations until late at night, the stories: seeing the love between you and your wife, the sweetness with which you spoke of your daughters. It was like being with family. The best hurricane of our lives.

I was happy, two years ago, as a guest at the Sanremo Casino and then at the Bicknell Museum in Bordighera, to be the proud spokesman of Bordighera Press, a precious gem born from the imagination of you, Anthony, and Fred. And it was in your town of Bordighera, where you were born in front of the house where Edmondo De Amicis lived (you told me this) that I was able to see the affection and admiration of your fellow countrymen, who in fact awarded you the "Parmurelu d'oru". They really hold you in high esteem, and I think that the reason for this, besides the pride they feel for the great professional achievements of their fellow citizen, is the pure and generous spirit that sets you apart.

Every time I needed professional advice or to have you read something of mine, and when I was going through a very delicate period at work and needed a mentor, you, like Anthony, were always there, and after all, in all these years I have always felt certain, as with Anthony, that "in case of danger" you would always be there. There are very few people in my life in whom I have such trust. And my relationship with my students is the result of a transitive property, a handover, a "copy & paste": from you and Anthony to me, from me to them.

Now, Ilaria wishes to add something.

Ti voglio bene, grande Paolo!

Ilaria's message.

My first memory of Paolo also coincides with the beginning of my American adventure or, rather, it precedes it. I met Paolo at the conference of Istituto Suor Orsola Benincasa in Naples in 1997... it was dedicated to the Italian-American dream. And Italian-American dream it has been, for me, also thanks to him.

Paolo accompanied us in our studies of the anthology *From the Margins*; he passed to me his love for Joseph Tusiani; he supported us in the first years of study abroad in Florence; he was part of the first ever *Italy in Transit* Symposium in 2017; he invited me for an Euliano Lecture at the University of Central Florida, followed by a wonderful reception that was held right at his home... all around a beautiful sculpture by Rosa that I still don't forget. Great Paolo, with your beautiful Ligurian accent, you are part of our history.

Thank you for everything and best wishes!

VIRGINIA PICCHIETTI

I was Paolo Giordano's student at Rosary College (now Dominican University, River Forest, Illinois), class of 1987. I had chosen Rosary for its Italian program, which Paolo had been instrumental in designing and building and which had an excellent reputation. When I was a senior in a high school in the Chicago area, Paolo came to present the program. I especially liked the study of literature but was uncertain of a career path. Paolo's description, coupled with an inspirational explanation of the value of languages and language education, convinced me of the importance of pursuing a degree in the field. With Paolo as my professor, I received an education that to this day informs my own approach to teaching.

Paolo's literature courses, such as the one on the modern novel and Dante's *Divina Commedia*, were grounded in rich cultural history. His class discussions were designed to guide us towards becoming keen and independent readers of literature. His questions asked us to probe a text's relationship to context, and to equally consider its aesthetic value as conveyor of meaning. I would go to Paolo's lessons excited to participate in discussion and further develop the skills of interpretation. Some of the moments that most inspired and formed me as a future professor of literature included the way in which Paolo incorporated art and art history into our conversations. By highlighting the interconnectedness of different art forms in mapping human experience, this approach helped me appreciate even more artists' use of the literary and visual arts to craft a response to the world. Paolo's courses not only prepared me for the intellectual demands of graduate school, but also for the challenges of designing my own courses. When I began teaching as a newly hired assistant professor of Italian in the fall of 1995, I referred back, for guidance, to Paolo's holistic curriculum and gentle and welcoming, yet structured method of leading discussions.

Today, as language programs are cut and even eliminated, the words I heard Paolo speak in high school resonate even more, as do his lessons at Rosary College. I can only hope that his legacy, channeled through to my students, will help them realize the importance of intercultural communication and the value of art as a powerful exploration of what it means to be human in dialogue with the world.

Grazie di cuore, Paolo!

Virginia Picchietti
The University of Scranton

Mark Pietralunga

Paolo Giordano's "Moveable Feast"

> *People were always limiters of happiness except for the very few that were as good as spring itself.*
> Ernest Hemingway

Over the forty plus years that I have known Paolo, I have had the great pleasure of spending time with him in a variety of settings, at numerous professional conferences, collaborating with him on scholarly projects, teaching on his study abroad program in Florence back in the early 1980s, and sharing experiences and strategies as chairpersons. Regarding the latter, I chuckle when I think back to one of Paolo's emails not long after he accepted the position of chair of the Department of Foreign Languages and Literatures at the University of Central Florida in 2004 and was learning to navigate in the world of the Florida legislature. He wrote: "So we are going to save all tenure track and tenured positions

[…] that is as long as the legislature does not impose any more cuts […] Ma *speriamo bene*. I used to be a very optimistic human being, then I came to Florida." Even if Paolo's optimism may have been slightly and momentarily tempered, he was always prepared to bring a little humor to your day with his "Buon divertimento" emails that many of his friends and colleagues may recall. They dealt with a wide range of topics that included "Great Rodney Dangerfield lines," "An analysis of hell ("Is Hell Exothermic or Endothermic?"), "Just a little humor to help ease the pain of your next trip to the pump," "Words of wisdom for my Republican friends," "Abbott and Costello's computer conversation," "Catholic parrots," and "A little levity is what is needed after our umpteenth hurricane."

As I reviewed my correspondence with Paolo over the years, I came across an email dated August 16, 2011, that included a photo of him, Anthony Tamburri, and me at the Trattoria Antichi Cancelli in the San Lorenzo quarter of Florence. The email was accompanied by the following words: "A photo taken by Rosa of the three of us *'a tavola.' Sembra che siamo sempre a tavola*." Paolo's seemingly simple statement not only is a reminder of the many enjoyable moments I have shared with him, but also it captures the convivial spirit that I have always associated with him. To be with Paolo, one feels, literally and figuratively, to be always "a tavola." While good food and wine are certainly two things that Paolo has taken great pride in, it is his ability to cultivate a congenial and nurturing environment that ultimately results in the sharing of ideas and forming meaningful bonds. He has been able to transfer that spirit of commensality into building relationships and creating a sense of community, whether it be as a director and dean of a premier study abroad program, the president of a major scholarly and educational organization, the chair of large and diverse academic departments, through his many collaborations as a publisher and editor, and as a builder of bridges between the Italian and the Italian American worlds.

To all this I say to Paolo: "Alla salute!"

Mark Pietralunga
Florida State University

COLLEEN RYAN

"IMPEGNO E GENTILEZZA": A NOTE OF APPRECIATION FOR
PROFESSOR PAOLO GIORDANO

A scholar, a leader, a mentor, a friend — these are just some of the roles attributable to Paolo Giordano and his contributions to the fields of Italian and Italian American studies for over fifty years. Distinguished by lengthy tenures at Rosary College (now, Dominican University), Loyola University, and the University of Central Florida, Paolo's career has demonstrated unwavering dedication to research, teaching, and service to the profession, and he has had a lasting impact on all of the academic communities to which he belongs. Beyond his status as beloved professor, esteemed colleague, and long-standing department chair, Paolo has been a pioneer in Italian American studies, an accountable spokesperson and editor, and a great champion for Italian language and culture through our national associations.

It is the combination of scholarship, advocacy, and humanity that make Paolo so memorable to me. His Italian Studies bibliographies, for example, were a staple for me as a graduate student, growing my familiarity with the cannon and critical works through this annual publication he organized both chronologically and thematically. Next, his co-edited *From the Margin, Writings in Italian Americana* marked my first formal experience with Italian American writing and cultural history. This volume prompted me for the first time to consider the role one's ancestry and upbringing may have had on one's professional trajectory. Third, Paolo's "Joseph Tusiani: The Man and His Work" not only deepened my appreciation for Tusiani's poetry but also urged me to reflect on the intercultural experiences of my own family.

Paolo's work in Italian American studies, developed in concert with his cherished co-authors Tamburri and Gardaphé, has therefore, led me to discover the bearing that my cultural heritage has had on my scholarly inquiries and personal identity. But most of all, Paolo & co. have modeled the essence and the beauty of professional collaborations driven by *impegno* and sustained by humor, kindness, and humility.

Colleen M. Ryan, Tufts University

Ann Verdone Saporito

Seems like a lifetime ago, but I never realized how my college Italian studies, led by Prof. Paolo Giordano, would have such an impact on my life. Through his teachings, his passion became our passion. We all fell in love with everything Rinascimento, Arte, Storia, ed Architettura, the most beautiful in the world.

I was a tag along and met the group in Firenze in 1979. To say It was Magical, is an understatement! To this day the memories and all the beauty, fill my heart with immeasurable joy! My favorite Boticelli art hangs in my home. My daughters went to Yellow Bar in Firenze for a pizza on a recent trip of theirs, where I celebrated my 22nd birthday back in 1979. Life comes full circle … they loved it!

My forever gratitude to you, Prof Giordano, for the gift of sharing your passion! You are a true gem! Words cannot describe what you mean to so many.

Con tantissimo affetto,
Ann Verdone Saporito '79 ⚜️❤️

Lyn Scolaro

Paolo, the Professional Love of My Life!

There are not enough words in both languages to express my gratitude and affection for you. As a young, excited freshman in college at Rosary College, seeking to become an Italian teacher as a non-native among all natives, you took me on an adventure ride that has yet to slow down at the station. You were my professor in all things Italian and taught me so much about art, history, architecture, and culture. You were an extension of my family to appreciate and to treasure the word, Heritage. You hired me to work in your office acquainting me with some of the greatest minds, Tamburri, Lettieri, Banchieri, and many more, who I quickly looked up to and still look up to, to honor as my professional heroes. You guided me into the "profession" through AATI beyond the classroom.

You believed in this young girl to push her to be the best. You made ONLY ME take a 20-page final exam before graduation because I was becoming a teacher, and my students deserved the best even though I already had a job. In this way, you commandingly taught me character. You expected more from me than I ever thought possible in myself. You looked out for me when I questioned my ability to pursue my career in and outside of my safe environment from study abroad to student trips.

You encouraged me to share my work with others by placing me on the AATI Midwest Board and eventually guiding me as President which was supposed to last two years and has lasted over 30. You also mentored me by example to share my work and to participate in conferences and seminars across the country and abroad. You demonstrated, and I followed, that this Italian stuff was a way of life and worth sharing every day. My passion was ignited by my parents, but you fueled the fire and what a lovely "falò" it is.

The greatest gifts of all have been your kindness, your friendship, your love. You've included me in your family. You're my lifelong, forever friend who is always just a phone call away. Your strength continues to amaze me and inspire me. I hope I have lived up to your expectations and that I have made and continue to make you proud to continue your teaching legacy.

With more love and gratitude than you will ever know, I wish you every blessing. Thank you for giving me a life I could have never dreamed possible and for loving me.

Ti voglio tanto tanto tanto bene.

Con infinito affetto,
Lyn
Cavaliere e Professoressa

Antonio Vitti

Before meeting Paolo Giordano personally I had heard about him with much esteem and affecttion from Prof. Edoardo Lebano, who had known him as a student, and over time a true friendship had been born between them, so when I met him in Erice at a conference I had organized on Mediterranean culture, I had the impression that I had always known him even though I had never met him, and that I was seeing an old and esteemed friend again.

The following day we went, together with my wife, to San Vito Lo Capo and I was able to witness directly: the kindness, friendliness, sense of humor and spontaneity of Paolo.

Over the years we met again at various AATI conferences and one summer at the Middlebury College summer program in Vermont. That summer director Giuseppe De Santis was with us to make a film with the students. Paul formed a very good relationship with De Santis and actively participated in the making of the project that Peppe wanted to call, "Bye Bye, Middlebury."

During these past years I have not seen Paolo again but I always maintained a great esteem for him and appreciated his academic initiatives and publications and I always continued to call Paolo!

Antonio Carlo Vitti

Maria Rosaria Vitti-Alexander

Dear Paolo,

Quite some time has passed, and re-reading the name Paolo Giordano brings back many but many memories! Those wonderful summers spent teaching together.

You and your family stayed downstairs while my children and I occupied the upstairs. We would meet for breakfast, and in the afternoons out and about with the children. Often when you saw me struggling with my two little boys you would offer me help. You would usually take one of the two, the older one, with you, and you would take long rides along the river, up and down ravines and lanes collecting pets and flowers, which my son would then bring me as gifts.

Paolo, after those wonderful summers we spent together, we never saw each other again. Our academic journey took us by different routes, our children are now grown, and we are grandparents.

We have not seen each other again, although I would love it if we could meet again and talk about the past.

Un fortissimo abbraccio, Paolo,
e buon compleanno, mio caro amico!

Maria Rosaria Vitti-Alexander, Ph.D.
Professor Emerita and Adjunct
World Languages and Cultures, Nazareth College

M. Stella Martorana Weber

I'm writing in reference to the greatest Italian professor I had during my time at Rosary College, River Forest, Il. During this time, circa 1980-82, he was my instructor, advisor, mentor and I may even add tormentor (said with much love and affection, oh the exams were killer.). It is Prof. Paolo Giordano who guided me into the greatest career of being an educator.

I had Prof. Giordano for many classes during the day. I remember having up to 3 classes with him during a full day. This happened because he was the Italian program. I never tired of him.

I even worked for him as a student assistant where he introduced me into the world of foreign language conferences. That being said, he molded me to be the best Italian teacher I could be.

It's because of Prof. Giordano that I was able to be hired as a notable Italian teacher. I could write many pages about my experiences with this great man. I saw him as a father bringing his young daughter to daycare, an educator and a friend. He lifted me up when I wanted to drop everything. His advice would carry me through some real rough times of being a student and real-life situations.

There aren't enough words that can express my gratitude for his direction, kindness and firmness to make me the professional that I needed to be.

Sinceri Auguri, Carissimo Professore Giordano. Ti auguro un mondo di felicità.

Con tanto affetto,
M. Stella Martorana Weber

Paolo and Rosa a spasso (photo courtesy of Peter Carravetta)

Anthony, Robert Viscusi, Peter, Giorgio Mariani, Paolo, Leonardo Bonomo, Donatella Izzo, Bellagio 2014
(photo courtesy of Peter Carravetta)

Part V

Photos

Paolo and Rosa

Michèle, Rosa, Paolo, Stephanie

Stephanie, David, Isabell, Beatrice, Paolo, Sophie, Michèle, John, Rosa

Fred and Paolo • Bellagio 2.0, 2018

Anthony, Peter, Paolo • Bellagio 2.0, 2018

Paolo, Anthony, Fred • 25 Years of Bordighera Press

October 28, 2024 • Anthony, Paul, Fred, Nicholas

In fall 2024, after 35 years of independent publishing, Bordighera Press was incorporated into the John D. Calandra Italian American Institute, Queens College, CUNY. In this conversation, the three co-founders, along with Bordighera editor Nicholas Grosso, discuss the history of the Press.

Afterword

Fred L. Gardaphe

Afterword

What we have in this volume, along with some of Paul's writings, are contributions by friends and colleagues, two categories I'm happy to say that I've enjoyed being in for over forty years. Because of our relationship, I've shied away from publicly commenting on his work in writing, but when *Ethnicity*, his book on Joseph Tusiani came out, I had to speak up, for besides Paul's insightful essays, the selection of Tusiani poems included were those I had first encountered in Tusiani's collection *Gente Mia*, originally published by the Italian Cultural Center of Stone Park.

Through Paul's work, new readers could learn that Tusiani is a master at capturing dimensions of the immigrant experience. The poet combines the knowledge of a well-versed scholar with the heart of an emotionally honed human to create formalistic poetry of the most ordinary of miracles and the most extraordinary of historical acts. Paul also showed us that the alienation themes that characterized the episodic writing of the early Italian/American novelists such as Pietro di Donato are crystallized in Tusiani's work. Through this work Tusiani takes on the responsibility of speaking for the earlier immigrants.

As Paul pointed out, "Tusiani shows the reader that the American cultural milieu has absorbed the superficial and stereotypical aspects of Italian immigrant culture while never understanding the true character of this populace.... It is up to the poet, who draws his inspiration from the injustice suffered by his people, to assure that their sacrifice will not be forgotten." Paul had gathered a representative collection of Tusiani's classic poetry that serves as an excellent introduction to this classic Italian American writer, making it an essential publication for those already familiar with this great poet's work. But there is more to Paolo Antonio Giordano than what meets the eye on the page and in person.

He is an Italianist; I am an Americanist. A long time ago, we were both working in the languages we weren't born with; I was trying to master Italian, and he was presenting his first talk on Italian American writers at a conference on Italian American Culture organized by Dominic Candeloro at Triton Jr. College, in River Grove, Illinois — my first college alma mater. I remember the date well because 1) it was my mother's birthday; 2) that morning one of my favorite authors, John Fante, died in California; and 3) I was there to introduce the keynote speaker who never came; and 4) it was the day I met Paul.

I was an assistant professor of English at Columbia College in Chicago, and Paul was an associate professor of Italian at Rosary College, a Dominican Catholic school close to where I had grown up. I think I was the only one in the room to really understand what Paul was talking about as he ventured into something I had never heard before — a formal lecture on Italian American writers. I had been immersed in reading the likes of Rose Basile Green, the scholar upon whose work Paul based his talk; I had worked with Dominic Candeloro's Italian Americans of Chicago collection of oral histories. I had read and met Tina DeRosa, Tony Ardizzone, but I had never heard anyone speak of Italian American literature in public.

I sat in the audience and was intrigued by his talk as I thought I had been the only one within at least a thousand-mile radius who had read Green's *The Italian American Novel: A Document of the Interaction of Two Cultures*, a groundbreaking book derived from her doctoral thesis. When I asked a question from the audience, his eyes lit up, as he too had thought he was the only one who cared enough about Green's work to use it in a formal presentation. During the session break I introduced myself, and he immediately did what Paul (and his wife Rosa) are apt to do if they're interested in you, he invited me to his home for dinner. You see, Paul is one who knows that work is not separated from life and is not something that needs to be done in isolation of the rest of a person's life. It would be the first of many times when we'd combine the good life with the academic life to make working a joy.

Since then, Paul and I have become great friends and colleagues, even though we've never worked in the same place, we have worked on the same projects and publications over the past forty-plus years; from conference sessions to conference directing, symposia, to publishing, editing, fundraising, project directing, you name it in the world of academia, and we've worked together in some way on it all. One thing I've learned about Paul is that he is a believer of quality and not quantity in most of the areas of his life. He's also one of the most accomplished administrators I've ever met, and I don't say this lightly. He has become a master at doing that work that must be done, especially when no one wants to do it. This, in my mind, is the power of Paolo and the legacy that he left when he had the brains to enter emeritus status. Most of what I've learned in terms of dealing with academic and cultural institutions have come from watching Paul negotiate his way out of some of the toughest personnel situations and into some of the most prestigious places for presenting ideas and work.

It was Paul who administratively led the way for the creation of Bordighera Press as it was he who introduced me to his friend Anthony Julian Tamburri a few years after he and I had met at the Triton College conference. Paul had organized a session in which the three of us gave papers on Italian American literature at a conference where we were accused, by professors of Italian, of creating a ghetto for American writers who just happened to be of Italian descent.

The three of us decided to find a way to publish our essays. It was Paul who, despite the cold and sometimes outright antagonistic reception of the three papers on Italian American writers that he, Anthony and I gave at in that Italian session at the Twentieth Century Literature Conference in Louisville in 1990, harnessed our energies and gathered us into to his office at Rosary College where we concocted a plan to expand our papers and publish our essays. Thus, began a search that grew into our anthology project which was rejected a number of times before it was published by Purdue University Press as *From the Margin: Writings in Italian Americana* (1991).

During the production and promotion of that anthology we met so many Italian American writers that we decided we would need a journal to keep the conversation alive and current. And so, even before the anthology appeared, we realized the need for a journal, especially since the only academic journal in Italian American studies, *Italian Americana* had suspended publication. When our pleas to take over responsibility for producing the journal, during which Paul, the only one of us to wear suits at the time, displayed his classic authoritative *bravado* in the face of professional and personal attacks, we decided we needed to create a new journal.

After requests for seed money were ignored or dismissed by every major Italian American group with a history of donating money, we lobbied the Fondazione Giovanni Agnelli, an Italian version of the Ford Foundation and were granted the money to start *Voices in Italian Americana*, which has since become a major forum for creative and critical writing in the field of Italian American Studies. As we were creating the journal, a lawyer from Rosary College suggested that we create an entity that would house the journal and enable us to do more in the future, if we desired. Thus, was born Bordighera Press, which became a home from which the publications would continue to flow to this day and rightly was named after Paul's hometown in Italy.

Over the years, I have come to depend on Paul as a friend, colleague, and fellow sports aficionado. Whenever possible we'd play a round of golf, watch football or simply sit back and enjoy a good meal. He joins the ranks of what I have come to call, the good professors, but beyond that he continues to be a student of life, looking for the best to share with the rest of us who have made it into his circle of friendship.

Grazie, fratello mio, for all you do and for what you've done to make my life better in so many ways.

Fred L. Gardaphe
Queens College and
John D. Calandra Italian American Institute

Index of Names

Arpino, Giovanni 102, 118

Baldini, Piero xii, xxii
Ballerini, Luigi 10
Barolini, Helen xxi, 3, 43, 45-6, 54-56, 59, 67-8,
Barthe, Roland 17
Bartoli, Girolamo 92
Basile-Green, Rose 11, 43, 66
Bellino Giordano, Rosa 5
Belloni, Antonio 95
Bertone, Giorgio 95
Bianchi, Fulvio 95-7
Boelhower, William 43, 50, 68
Bolzeta, Francesco 92
Bona, Mary Jo 5
Brugnolo, Gioacchino 92
Buzzati, Dino 19, 26, 37

Calabretta-Sajder, Ryan v
Campisi, Paul 55, 68
Caneo, Giuseppe 92-3
Capucci, Martino 96
Carravetta, Peter 9-11, 13, 17, 37-8, 40
Carrera, Alessandro 10
Cebà, Ansaldo 73, 96
Cecchetti, Giovanni 16-19, 22-26, 35, 38-40

Chiabrera, Gabriello vi, xx, 73-97
Chiappelli, Fredi 19, 38
Ciambelli, Bernardino 6, 123
Cian, Vittorio 96
Cicognini, Iacopo 84
Cipolla, Gaetano xi
Coleridge, Samuel 99
Columbus, Christopher 77, 79-80, 91, 145
Cordiferro, Ricardo 7
Cornaro, Luigi 74
Corradini, Marco 96
Corti, Maria 99-101, 105, 114, 118
Croce, Benedetto 73, 79, 96

Dagostino, Guido 50, xi
D'Alfonso, Antonio xi
Dandolo, Enrico 77
D'Angelo, Pascal 7, 11, 46-50, 68
Dante 47, 82
Dante, Micahel x
de Amicis, Edmondo 3
de'Dottori, Carlo 74
De Lemene, Francesco 74
De Maria, Bianca 106, 118
de' Medici, Cosimo 79, 84-5, 90, 92

De Nicola, Francescso 4, 12
de Ronsard, Pierre 74
De Sanctis, Francesco 84, 96
di Biasio, Rodolfo 3
di Donato, Pietro 42, 45, 67-8
Dinale, Rita 10
Dolci, Roberto xi, xv,
Durante, Francesco vi, 6-8, 12

Fante, John 45, 67
Fenoglio, Beppe vi, xx, 99-119
Ferrari, Severino 95
Filippo, Giacomo 94, 100
Fontanella, Lugi 10, 12, 38, 40

Gardaphé, Fred vi, xii, xviii, xxii, 5, 12, 38, 43, 45, 47, 50, 59, 68-9
Garofalo, Piero 37
Getto, Giovanni 114
Gibby, Sian v-vi, xix
Giunta, Edvige 54-5, 67-8, 105
Giustiniani, Pier Giuseppe 73
Grignani, Maria Antonietta 100, 105
Grosso, Nicholas v, 178

Guidi, Alessandro 74

Hicks, D. Emily 17, 37-8

Iannaco, Carmine 96

Jori, Giacomo 96

Kotsaftis, Maria 54, 68

Lapolla, Garibaldi 43-4
Leake, Elizabeth 38
Lettieri, Micahel 20, 23-4, 38
Lopreato, Joseph 55, 69

Mancini, Albert vi, xi-xii, xix-xx, xxii, 97
Mangione, Jerre 43-5, 68
Mannucci, Francesco Luigi 97
Manunzio, Paolo 74
Marabini, Claudio 101, 119
Maragoni, Gian Piero 97
Marazzi, Martino 8-10, 12, 39
Marchand, Jean-Jacques 69
Marini, Quinto 97
Marescotti, Giorgio 92, 95
Marino, Giambattisa 73, 75-6, 92
Mauro, Walter 100, 119
Mazzuchelli, Chiara v, 6

Mazzuchelli, Samuel
    Charles v, 6
Meddemmen, John 100
Menzini, Benedetto 74
Merola, Nicola 95
Merry, Bruce 100
Murassana, Geronima 74
Muret, Marc Antoine 74

Neri, Ferdinando 97

Orpin, Giovanni 101

Papini, Maria Carla 18, 39
Parise, Goffredo 5
Pascoli, Giovanni 3
Patriarca, Gianna 9
Pavoni, Giuseppe 92-3
Payne, Roberta L. 18
Perez-Firmat, Gustavo 15, 39
Periconi, James 12
Petrarch 82
Petrillo, Rayomond 39
Pettener, Emmanuele 10
Pieri, Mariza 97
Pietralunga, Mark v
Pirandello, Luigi 3
Potter, Halley viii, xv
Prezzolini, Giuseppe 5-6, 11
Puzo, Mario 42, 45, 67, 69

Redi, Francesco 74
Renga, Dana 38
Rimanelli, Giose 9, 67
Rinuccini, Ottavio 73
Ruberto, Laura E. ix, xv, 16, 39

Sanfilippo, Carla Maria 100
Savoia, Carlo Emanuele I 75, 89
Savoia, Emanuele Filiberto 77, 89
Sbrocchi, Leonard xi
Serra, Illaria 8, 13
Sciorra, Joseph vi, ix, xv, 16, 39
Siani, Cosma 39
Sisca, Alessandro 7
Soldati, Mario 5, 15
Speroni, Sperone 74
Strozzi, Gian Battisita 73

Tamburri, Anthony Julian vi, xv, 10, 12-3, 15, 38-9, 43, 55, 57-8, 69
Tasso, Torquato 74, 87
Testi, Fulvio 74, 100, 102, 105
Titi, Roberto 73
Tomasoni, Piera 100
Tusiani, Joseph 3, 9, 13, 16, 26-9, 39-40, 46, 60-1, 69

Valesio, Paolo 10, 13, 15-6, 34, 38, 40, 43, 45-6, 67, 70
Van Doren, Carl 49
Vazzoler, Franco 94-5, 97
Verdicchio, Pasquale 16
Viscusi, Robert vi, 40, 43, 70

Ward, Daniel 118
West, Rebecca 19, 26, 40
Winwar, Frances 9

DIASPORA

As "diaspora" is the dispersion or spread of people from their original home-land, this book series takes its name in the intellectual spirit of willful dispersion of subject matter and thought. It is dedicated to publishing those studies and creative works that in various and sundry ways speak to or offer new methods of analysis and/or articulations of the Italian diaspora.

Carmelo Fucarino. *Two Italian Geniuses in New York: Broken American Dreams.* ISBN 978-1-955995-05-4. 2023

Anthony Julian Tamburri, ed. *Re-Thinking* The Godfather *50 Years Later.* ISBN 978-1-955995-06-1. 2024

Anthony Socci. *United We Stand. Pre WW II-Chronicles of the Italian Colony of Stamford.* ISBN 978-1-955995-07-8. 2024

Antonio D'Alfonso. *I Could Have Been a Contender. (On Five Films).* ISBN 978-1-955995-09-2. 2024

Antonio Vitti and Anthony Julian Tamburri, eds. *Studi mediterranei: bellezze e misteri. Mediterranean Studies: Beauty and Mystery.* ISBN 978-1-955995-10-8. 2024

Luigi Fontanella. *Bertgang. Fanatasia onirica.* Translation by Michael Palma. ISBN 978-1-955995-11-05. 2025. Poetry

Mark Saba. *The Shoemaker.* ISBN 978-1-955995-12-2. 2025. Fiction

Anthony Julian Tamburri, ed. *Living Biculturalism, Writing Transculturalism: Essays in Honor of Luigi Fontanella.* ISBN 978-1-955995-13-9. 2025

Antonio Vitti and Anthony Julian Tamburri, eds. *Studi mediterranei: bellezze e misteri. Cultura mediterranea: variazioni su un tema.* ISBN 978-1-955995-15-3. 2025

CASA LAGO PRESS EDITORIAL GROUP

David Aliano	Donatella Izzo
Leonardo Buonomo	John Kirby
William Boelhower	Chiara Mazzucchelli
Ryan Calabretta-Sajder	Emanuele Pettener
Nancy Carnevale	Mark Pietralunga
Stephen J. Cerulli	Joseph Sciorra
Donna Chirico	Ilaria Serra
Fred Gardaphé	Anthony Julian Tamburri
Paolo A. Giordano	Sabrina Vellucci
Nicolas Grosso	Leslie Wilson

from Casa Lago Press

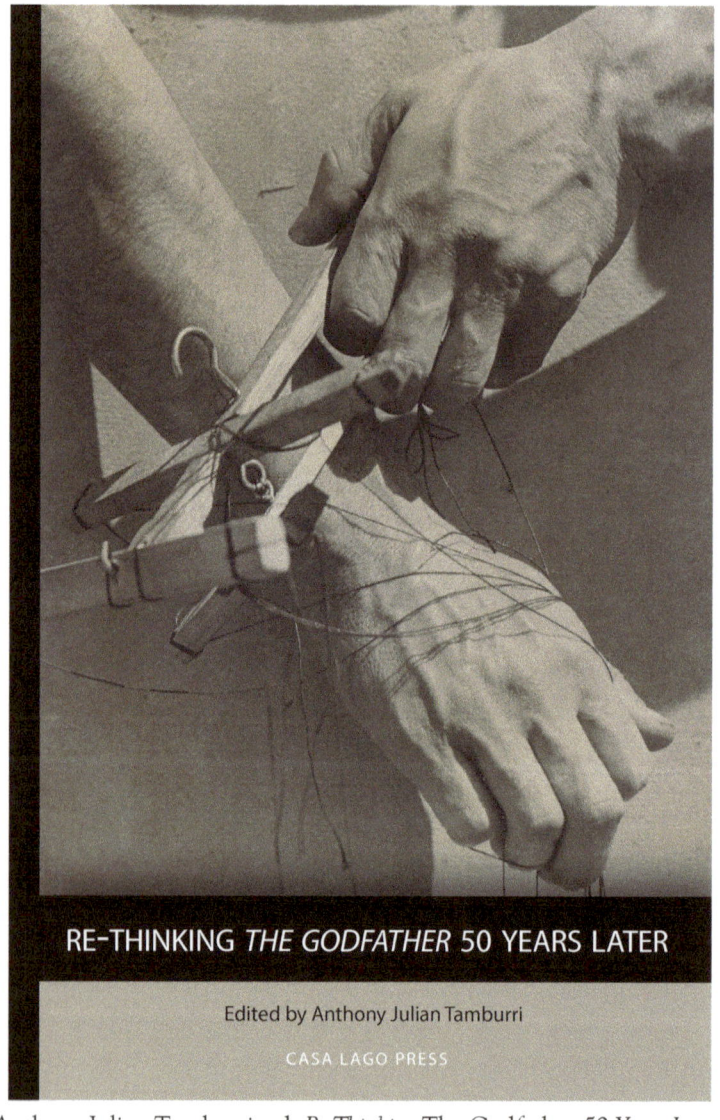

Anthony Julian Tamburri, ed. *Re-Thinking* The Godfather *50 Years Later*.
ISBN 978-1-955995-06-1. 2024

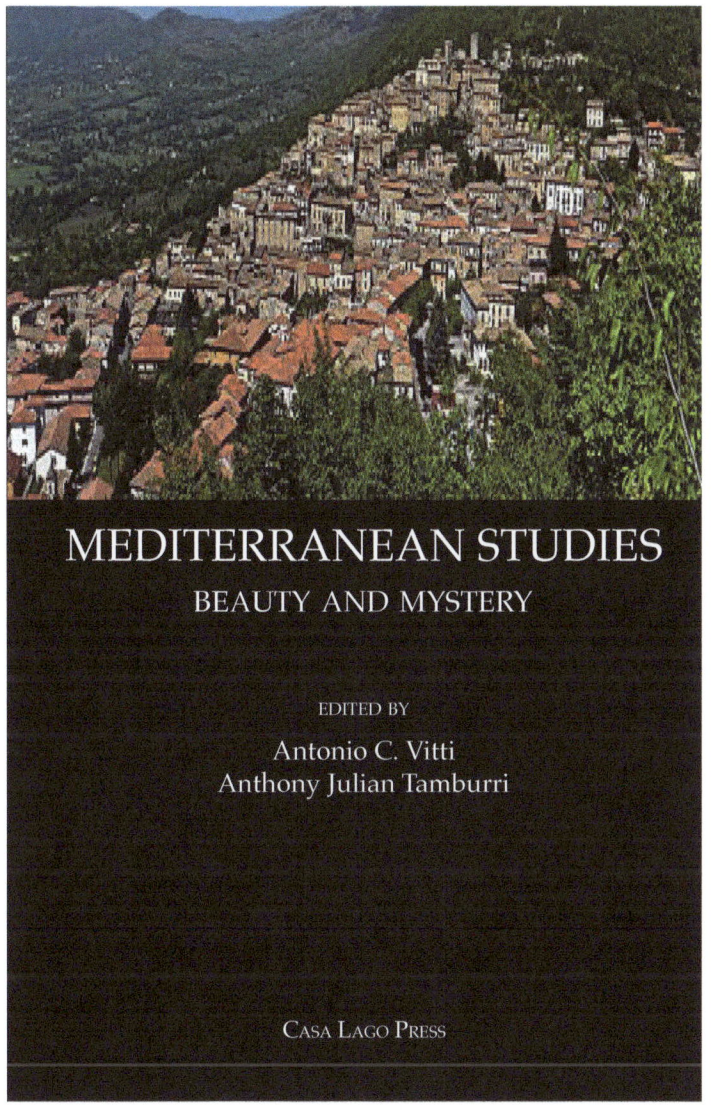

Antonio Vitti and Anthony Julian Tamburri, eds. *Studi mediterranei: bellezze e misteri. Mediterranean Studies: Beauty and Mystery.* ISBN 978-1-955995-10-8. 2024

Luigi Fontanella

Bertgang
An Oneiric Phantasy

Translation and Introduction
by Michael Palma

CASA LAGO PRESS

Luigi Fontanella. *Bertgang. Fanatasia onirica*. Translation by Michael Palma. ISBN 978-1-955995-11-05. 2025. Poetry

Mark Saba. *The Shoemaker*. ISBN 978-1-955995-12-2. 2025. Fiction

www.ingramcontent.com/pod-product-compliance
Lightning Source LLC
Chambersburg PA
CBHW042043240426
43667CB00048B/2964